When Hindsight is 30-30

by

Sam Welch

Printed in the United States of America

Second Edition 2017

I9781096809098

Other books by this author:

Tecumqua

What's Your Problem Cowboy?

Contents

Foreword

Who am I that Sam should ask me to provide insight into his story revealing life's surprises and spiritual growth on a personal journey directed by God's love? For me, Sam's story plucked a familiar chord. I'm just a friend, someone else who has struggled at times with life so hurtful that only God could understand and remedy. And I suspect I'm pretty much like everyone else, just a speck of humanity struggling with choices every day, getting shaped and reshaped. Older now, in the autumn of my life, I remember moments that made differences, crossroads where forgiveness by me and for me needed to be real, in God's grace. Sam's sharing of his journey has encouraged me to remember my own journey, especially the choices that made a difference. We all live within a fabric of victories and tragedies. It's hard to say how often we get lost in weaving our own stories, forgetting how important each moment and choice can be, choices that continue to shape and color the future. Sam's journey reveals a moment of un-forgiveness; its silent impact through nineteen years, being replaced by a simple act of love facing the truth – reminiscing about forgiveness and love being part of his story all along, but missing one fundamental moment needing the remedy that God illuminated as a simple choice--not too late for Sam to make. It's an interesting story portraying a portion of a man's life, sometimes funny, sometimes tragic, revealing life's illusion of strength and fortitude, finding simple but real victory in the reality of God's wisdom. Jesus Christ said, "With God all things are possible." In his book Sam shares a journey and some of the

1

seemingly impossible challenges he faced, living the best way he knew how, trying to make the right choices, not as a preacher or prophet, but as one under the watchful eye of his Creator. Possibly, some may consider Sam responsible for taking another's life or for other misdeeds, which are now in the past. Like a spiritual Robinson Crusoe Sam has discovered the bigger footprints in the sand and a real personal relationship with God. I have come to know Sam as a man living his faith, strong enough, I believe, to walk into the desert toward destinations unknown -- knowing Jesus Christ is with him and has always been there. Such a concept may seem easy to discuss, but each life is a challenging journey to decipher unto its own end, priceless but with value lived. Sometimes we are lucky enough to share such a personal journey as Sam's, helping us to appreciate God's presence in our

own lives. This book was one such experience for me.

Gib Hice

Prologue

The guest speaker was most likely in his early seventies yet well preserved. He was mild mannered in appearance and far too intellectual for a missionary who had spent the past thirty years spreading

The Gospel in the wilds of Africa. I had pictured him weather-beaten and rough. My expectations had probably been swayed by childhood fantasies from Rudyard Kipling and Edgar Rice Boroughs.

I welcomed the opportunity to escape the hum-drum drawl of rural Southern Oregon, to venture beyond the mundane into the endless reaches of the exotic where grassy plains watered by the runoff from Mt. Kilimanjaro provided life to scattered herds of giraffes and zebra.

My hopes were dashed when the missionary announced, "I had planned to speak about Africa, but God wants me to talk about un-forgiveness!"

I dismissed my disappointment. *If God wanted to address un-forgiveness then someone needed to hear it, but certainly not me! I held no grudge.*

The missionary cleared his throat and began, "Un-forgiveness can keep you from reaching your full potential, it can stunt your mental, spiritual and even your physical growth. Un-forgiveness can keep you from becoming what God intended for you to be. It can be passed down thru families with each generation worse than the one that preceded it, and It has led to the destruction and downfall of entire nations."

Sam Welch

He took a sip from a glass of water on the pulpit and continued, "Here in America we have what we call dysfunctional families. The root cause of this dysfunction is, you guessed it, un-forgiveness, and most commonly divorce!"

He asked for a show of hands from people who had been divorced.

From the second row on the far left, where my wife and I were seated, I glanced around the sanctuary. My eyes fastened on the third, fourth, and fifth rows across the aisle where the *fabulous forties and fifties group* sat. They were older married couples within the church, a close-knit bunch of friends who golfed, bowled, hiked and went on picnics together. Most of them were *transplants* who had sold small houses in California for outrageous amounts and retired in Oregon where their equity could afford mansions.

I didn't mean to be judgmental, but every hand within the group was lifted, and I was astounded.

The missionary stepped down from the platform and centered himself in front of the far aisle where the hands had been raised. He continued with, "The best way to forgive someone who has offended you is to speak to that person face to face. In some cases the offender has passed away, and forgiving them may be a little more difficult. Wives, this may not go over well with your husband but you may need to sit down with your ex over a cup of coffee and talk without your husband present! In some cases this may not be possible because there are some people that you just can't talk to. If you can talk to your ex then you must be careful not to accuse or start an argument, you should also make it clear that it's about forgiveness, not reconciliation. Husbands, this may not go over well with your wife, but you may need to sit down with your ex in order to forgive them, and they may need to forgive you as well…"

He paused and turned, cocking his head as if a strange odor had filled the air. Raising the index finger on his right hand, he followed it across the front of the church exclaiming as he walked, "It may not be an ex-husband or an ex-wife at all!"

When he reached the empty chair in front of me he turned again and leaned across it. Placing his index finger in front of my nose, he exclaimed, "it could be that girl who dumped you for another guy nineteen years ago!"

I nearly swallowed my tongue. I knew exactly what he was talking about, and I knew that he could not have known about it by any natural means.

An irritating numbness gripped me, a throbbing agony mysteriously devoid of the pain that it seemed to need in order to be valid coursed through my body. Sweat welled on my forehead. Before I knew it the missionary was gone—back to the other side of the church where he resumed preaching.

His sermon seemed distant—his words unintelligible.

My wife leaned toward me and uttered, "Maybe you should call her—sit down and talk with her."

Her advice struck me like a kick to the head when I was already down. "Oh yeah! That'll go over like a led balloon, won't it?" I snapped, baffled that my wife would ever vouch for such a thing, and after a few shushes from people behind me, I added in a softer tone, "if I do I'll spare you the details."

I wiped the sweat from my forehead and struggled mentally for answers. *The missionary couldn't have known anything about my life—it had to be a God thing, and since it was a God thing I had to act on it.*

Chapter One

C all her! How could I call her? What would I say? *That a missionary, whom I'd never met, picked me out of a crowd and said that I should call the girl who dumped me nineteen years ago in order to forgive her? Yeah right!*

I wasn't happy about it but I had to call her, I had a mandate from God!

I could see her lovely face in my mind, her long flowing golden-brown hair with its angelic glimmer glistening in the sun, silhouetting her shapely form. I could almost hear her voice.

Had it been nineteen years? It seemed less. I subtracted the years to see if the numbers meshed. It took a moment, a long moment, but as near as I could tell the missionary had nailed it! Nineteen years to the very month, perhaps the very day, a day buried deep in the recesses of my mind.

*

I returned in my mind to that day in October of 1974. The weather was calm, the air—mild, the sky was a cloudy blue. It was an ordinary day like any other day, and yet it would become the coldest day of my life.

I had called Shellie the night before, knowing she'd moved on, although I continued to pray for that off-chance that she would change her mind.

"Why are you calling me?" She demanded.

"I just needed to hear your voice," I replied.

"I don't need to hear yours!" Her tone was venomous, and then it softened, "but I need you to bring back my albums and photo."

The following morning as I pulled into Shellie's driveway I noticed her parent's car was gone, a fancy sports car was parked in its place.

I took the albums and photo to the front door and knocked. I could hear the sound of footsteps within. Moments later Shellie answered the door in her bathrobe, her face adorned with lipstick, mascara, and eye shadow, all in the right places. She looked as good as I had ever seen her, although it seemed strange that she was still in her bathrobe.

"Won't you come in?" she asked.

Her politeness stunned me. I knew better, and as I extended the albums and photo I said, "no, I just came to bring these back, and by the way, I didn't break the glass in the picture frame. I don't know how that happened."

"Oh please come in," she insisted, grabbing my arm in an almost desperate manner that made no sense, and left me bewildered.

"Okay, but just for a minute," I heard myself say.

After handing her the albums and photo I followed her into the living room.

Seated on the couch was a lanky young man with bad facial acne. His eyes followed her as she crossed the room to the coffee table. A half-smirk formed on his face as if he knew something that I was not aware of.

Shellie set the albums and picture down and motioned to the young man on the couch. "Steve, this is Sam—Sam—Steve."

Steve stood to his feet, towering over my mere five eleven. He offered his hand.

"Nice to meet you Steve," I lied, considering as I took his hand that I was relinquishing the girl I loved with a simple handshake. I pondered briefly the strange numbness I felt within. Despite the magnitude of the situation I had no tears, no rage, even my broken heart seemed subdued. I wanted only a dignified way to excuse myself.

I had just released his hand when Shellie threw herself into his arms. They kissed passionately. Not the casual passion of two lovers embracing and caressing, but the moaning, lip smacking, tongue tangling passion of

Sam Welch

starving ravenous lions, slurping down the steaming carcass of a freshly killed gazelle.

I was the gazelle!

I turned to leave, trying with all my strength to maintain my failing composure, tripping here, catching myself there. Somewhere between the house and my car I fell to my knees and lost my breakfast.

*

The signs had been posted several months earlier—the signs leading to our break-up. I should have seen it coming when her parents sat me down at the kitchen table. I knew something was amiss when they remained standing.

Her mother, Joan began, "You're probably wondering why we're having this talk." I glanced at Henry and back at Joan, their eyes shared a sincere, almost angry quality.

"I think you're about to tell me," I replied, knowing well it would be something I didn't want to hear.

"Yes we are! Recently we've become aware of your intentions to marry our daughter." Joan raised her eyebrows and glared at me as though I were the neighbor child caught with grubby hands in the cookie jar.

I nodded a yes. To do otherwise would be to deny my love, and that I could not do.

"You are how old now?"

"Eighteen, almost nineteen," I told her, biting my tongue and forcing my face to relax in order to hide my thoughts. *I knew she was going to play the age card. I felt it coming, and here it was, that line of thought that equates age with wisdom, and youth with stupidity, always served with a hint of jealousy by the older crowd since youth is wasted on the young. My best defense was to feign respect, after-all, the helpless kitten look had never served me well.*

"And how long have you been going with our daughter?"

"A little over three years." I felt a slight quiver in my voice, a common occurrence after catching myself in a half truth:

8

During those three years Shellie had broken our steady several times in order to date other guys only to reinstate the relationship after each date to prevent me from dating other girls.

"Other guys" had been her parent's suggestion to keep her from being tied down. What they really meant was that I wasn't good enough for their daughter.

"And how do you intend to support our daughter and future grandchildren?"

"I've been working for a logging outfit, setting chokers, bucking logs, cutting right-of-way, blasting stumps…"

"Yes, but that's seasonal!" she interrupted, clearly irritated with more than just my answer.

I glanced at Henry, his expression mirrored Joan's sentiments while his silence baffled me. *He was probably holding his tongue to keep from over-reacting.*

Joan picked up with, "What do you intend to do for a profession, for a life's work?"

"I'm going to write," I announced with all the certainty I could muster, fearing Joan would counter with enough venomous ridicule to stifle my fragile dreams.

"Write what?" she almost shouted, "write poems, newspapers? Write what?"

"Books," I replied calmly despite my shakiness, "I intend to write books!"

"That's all we wanted to know." Joan looked at Henry, they shook their heads making it obvious that their minds were made up. They had tried me and found me unworthy. I walked away feeling fragmented and misunderstood, wishing I could have said something meaningful in my own defense, yet knowing that words cannot penetrate closed minds and hardened hearts, and that the doors had closed on my youthful romance.

Chapter Two

Nineteen years had come and gone, and a lot of water had passed under that bridge, some of it tainted, but not all. I was happily married. I had a beautiful, intelligent wife, and four wonderful children.

I flashed upon the missionary's words, "Un-forgiveness will prevent you from becoming what God intends for you to be." I had dreamt of becoming a writer, but I was a millworker.

As I reached for the phone several thoughts gripped me, almost convincing me to withdraw my hand in fear. What if a jealous husband answers and demands to know why I am calling his wife? What if Shellie answers and doesn't want to talk?

Blocking my concerns, like one would hold his nose to down a shot of castor oil, I held my breath, then I picked up the phone and dialed information. When the operator answered I asked if there was a Shellie Noble in Crescent City, California. The operator gave me a number. I hung up, held my breath again, and dialed. The phone rang twice. A voice from the past uttered "hello."

I exhaled and drew a hasty breath. "Hi Shellie, this is…"

"Sam!" To my surprise her interruption was upbeat—encouraging. "I recognized your voice. To what do I owe this pleasure, after all these years?"

"Well…" Reeling from her positive response, I searched my mind for the right words. I didn't know how to explain the missionary thing, and for a moment I felt as though I was staring at a pile of wadded-would-be letters thrown at a corner wastebasket, each representing a failed attempt to find the right words to explain myself. "Uh, I've been thinking lately about forgiveness, and I thought it would be nice if you and I could sit down and visit over a coke or something."

"That would be wonderful. Where do you live now?" Her voice aroused within me memories of youth and hope, and naturally so, it was a voice that once defined love—first love to a teenage boy—a boy that still lived somewhere deep inside of me.

"Woodville, I live in Woodville, been here since eighty three," I said.

"How often do you go to the coast?"

"I'll be diving and spear fishing in the ocean near Brookings on Saturday.

"Diving?"

"Scuba diving," I replied, "it's something I picked up in the Navy. I'll tell you about it later. I'll leave here around seven, it takes me about two hours to get there."

"You've slowed down in your old age, you used to drive like…"

"Don't say it, I know, although my accelerator foot still gets itchy now and then."

"Two hours eh? That would put you in Hiouchi around nine. There's a gas station with a restaurant there, it's a great place to sit over a coke. It will be wonderful to catch up on what's happened over the past—how long has it been?"

"Nineteen years, a week, and two days," I heard myself say, instantly regretting how desperate I must have sounded, *as if I couldn't have waited another day!*

"Oh yeah, nineteen years, seventy two hours, fifteen minutes, and forty two seconds, but who's counting?" She giggled and added, "Has it been that long?

I suppressed my urge to laugh in order to keep my train of thought. "I know where that restaurant is, I'll see you around nine," I said, adding, "and yes it has it's been that long."

Sam Welch

We exchanged goodbyes, and I felt a deep relief as I hung up the phone. I couldn't help thinking how our conversation, her humor—my laughter was just like the conversations that two innocent kids shared together nineteen years earlier.

Chapter Three

When Friday night rolled around I called my Dive partner to let him know I wouldn't make it for the morning dive because I had to meet an old girlfriend, but I would make the afternoon dive.

I knew George would stretch the matter out of shape, adding his own hilarious spin to my words. He was one of my best sources of entertainment, all I had to do was give him the ammo.

"So you're gonna' catch a nooner with an old fling eh?" he joked.

"That's not the case George, it's about forgiveness."

He let out a chuckle with a tone that fell somewhere between sinister and skeptical. "You go ahead, I'll make the morning dive without you. See ya' in the afternoon, and don't name it after me."

*

Saturday morning I arose early and loaded my truck, carefully checking each item of dive gear to make sure I had it all. The song of the birds seemed more vibrant than I recalled, as they whistled their lament to the end of a long summer. The leaves were yellower, the air with its bite soothed me reminding me of the hunt and the joy of fall mornings of years past.

After tying my ocean kayak onto the lumber rack I was ready to go although something inside me was less than anxious, almost hesitant. I slid into the cab and sat for a moment examining my feelings. I thought that I had settled this matter in my mind years ago. There was no grudge, at least none that I was aware of. This was a God thing, I was doing it for him. Ironically I was aware that He was doing it for me. I leaned my head against the cold steering wheel and breathed, "Thank you Lord."

The old truck started just like it always had, and before I knew it I was on my way.

Sam Welch

The forested mountains and waterfalls along 199 that had become so commonplace, stood out like never before, and I found myself neither nervous nor anxious, but very content.

I drove no faster than I would on any other day, averaging perhaps ten miles over the speed limit, seldom slowing for corners, fast enough to tempt the cops, but not provoke them.

I gave little thought to my meeting with Shellie it would be what it was meant to be, an opportunity for me to forgive a grudge if I did indeed hold one. Granted, I had gone a little crazy in the years that followed our breakup, but I had long since recovered, or had I?

The miles flew by like a dream, a dream of crystal-green ocean and schools of large black rock fish begging to be taken. The dream was enhanced by the feint scent of salt air that filtered through the small opening in my side window. The yellow road lines seemed like dots passing beneath my bumper, and the hours, like minutes. Before I knew it I had reached Hiouchi.

I pulled off the road and into a parking space.

As I entered the restaurant I sensed the aroma of the grill. The mild buzz of conversation from a handful of scattered patrons mingling with the casual sound of background music generated a pleasant atmosphere.

A chubby woman sprang from one of the tables and hurried to meet me, her hair was cropped and greying. "Sam!" She threw her arms around me, and I, in reluctant disbelief, hugged her neck. After the hug she stepped back. Clinging to my sleeves she looked me over. "You haven't changed a bit in all these years. You look great!"

Her voice was all that remained of the girl of my past. I wanted to demand, *What have you done with Shellie?* But I eluded to, "So-so do you!

When Hindsight is 30-30

But your beautiful hair. What happened to your beautiful long, flowing hair?"

14

"It's so much easier to manage like this," she said, raising a hand to the back of her head, and giving it a pat.

"It looks nice anyway," I quickly dismissed my initial shock. It was good to see her, and I felt my lips tightening into a half-smile, the kind of pseudo smile your dog gives you when you return home after a long day at work without that doggy treat.

"You liar!" She chuckled. "Come and sit down." Turning, she motioned to her table. I followed and sat down opposite her.

She leaned forward anxiously, half giggling, half talking, "How is your mother, Irene?"

"She's fine."

"And Bob?"

"Same old Bob, hasn't changed a bit, still rules the roost the same way he has since he moved in and took over the pride. He still pounds his knife and fork on the table when dinner's late, but Mom seems happy with him and that's what counts."

"How are your brother and sister?"

"They're both well."

"And your cousins, Erwin and Warren?"

I forced a serious look. "Warren turned down twenty six football scholarships and joined the Marine Corps. He's been married and divorced several times, and Erwin married a black girl and had to give up his membership in the K.K.K."

She giggled. "You're kidding, right?"

I allowed the smile to return to my face. "We all have one of those cousins, don't we?"

"I heard you joined the Navy." Her expression was more serious but she kept the smile. "What was that like?"

"I spent years overseas in the sweltering heat dreaming of Southern Oregon fog and round-eye'd girls." I chuckled. "I think if I had it to do over again I wouldn't join, but hindsight is always twenty-twenty, or so they say." "Your hindsight is more like thirty-thirty." She laughed and

15

continued with, "You were always outrunning cops or in some altercation. Your chances of survival were probably better in the military, in fact it's a wonder you never got in trouble or even killed, but that's neither here nor there." An anxious smile formed on her face, her words and breathing reminded me of staccato notes between brief rests. A glimmer seemed to flash in her eye. "Catch me up on the years and the miles. Tell me about your life. I can hardly wait to hear it."

I flashed back on my life. Was it long, or brief? In retrospect it seemed like a combination of the two, a surreal conglomeration of events that any sane person would deem more lie than truth. I wasn't sure at first what to tell and what to omit, and although discretion had never been my greatest virtue, I found myself gazing across the table with my mouth open wide enough to swallow my foot.

Chapter Four

I enlisted in the Navy in the winter of seventy-four. I joined hoping to escape the pain of a broken heart, although the allure of almost three hundred dollars a month along with room and board had some bearing on my decision. I signed a contract with my grandmother to purchase her house in the Southern Oregon coastal town of Brookings, allotting her two hundred and fifty dollars a month, and allowing her to live rent free in the house while I purchased it. After taxes, I was left with only a few dollars for personal wants and needs.

By the spring of seventy-five I was stationed at the Subic Bay Naval Station in the Philippines. The Viet Nam war was ending and the evacuation was underway. The refugees were being processed on Grande Island in the center of the bay.

I was assigned to the admin department at Receiving Station.

RecSta, as it was called was the asshole of the base, situated, like the embarrassment that it was, a mile from the main station, with high cyclone fences which surrounded a network of barracks for transients, and a detention facility for lesser criminals and "legal holds."

The station was run like a prisoner of war camp by the Master-at-Arms, a rag-tag bunch of billyclub wielding thugs, headed by a Master Chief Petty Officer who was focused on retirement and did his best to distance himself from job related conflicts.

Ruling over the compound with an iron fist, was an elderly mustang lieutenant who feigned and often boasted of his own insanity. I thought he played the part well.

Several administrative workers had been pulled from the office to process Vietnamese refugees which left a skeleton crew to handle mountains of paperwork. We worked a thirty-two hour shift followed by sixteen hours off, which afforded us little time for sleep and recreation.

Sam Welch

As a seaman apprentice I was placed under the charge of a third class petty officer who expected me to do his work as well as my own. The rest of my superiors and the Master-at-Arms treated me like one of the detainees. They called me "Squirrel." I didn't know what it meant, but I knew it was derogatory.

Wilson, a black first class petty officer, served as one of the Masterat-Arms. He also served as the base karate instructor. Each morning after muster Wilson followed me across the grinder, kicking at my head to see how close he could come without connecting, missing sometimes by inches, but occasionally grazing my cheek or hairline. I could always hear it coming, telegraphed by his rendition of the Bruce Lee squeal that he released before each kick.

Sometimes it was multiple kicks in rapid succession, sometimes from the front, occasionally from the side. Once or twice he mixed it up with a round-house and some crazy looking sideways hop on one leg with the other extended at face level, my face level.

I never challenged him, never cared to. I just intended to keep my nose clean and not make waves.

Wilson's foot came a little close one day, clipping the side of my head. His friends were the first to notice, laughing and pointing at me as I rubbed my stinging cheek.

Wilson followed with, "You're lucky that didn't connect, squirrel!"

"No you're lucky, Wilson!" I blurted thoughtlessly, realizing after the fact that my words presented a challenge, and only then wishing I could call them back, but it was too late, Wilson's expression had changed, and I had to stand my ground.

Realizing I had gone beyond the point of return I decided to fully commit, "You're lucky you didn't connect, Wilson!"

I was never good at bluffing, I'm sure he could see the fear in my face—his friends could see it, they laughed me to scorn.

In a tone cooler than Dirty Harry, he slurred, "What did you just say to me?"

I considered an explanation, but humor seemed a better option. I mustered my deaf-mute voice, mimicking sign language with my hand, "hyou def or tomtin?"

A lightning heel struck the side of my head. I think it was right after signing with my middle finger. That was a mistake, I could see it in retrospect, but hindsight was—well, maybe mine was thirty-thirty.

The kick, that followed almost knocked me silly, and may have loosened some of my teeth. I might not have grabbed his ankle intentionally, I was pretty stunned, but I grabbed it none-the-less, and held it chest level.

Wilson threw several punches in an effort to make me release his ankle, at least one of them tagged me, but I knew that if I let go I was dead meat. I reinforced my grip with both hands and raised his ankle shoulder high.

My continual forward movement forced him backwards and kept him off balance, preventing him from hitting me.

I turned his ankle this way and that, steering him as I would a car while he hopped on one leg.

Forcing him to hop around angered him and made him look silly, but it allowed me time to recover from his kick and to regain my senses.

When I thought he had hopped long enough, I wrenched his foot hard and kicked his hopping leg from under him. He fell face first to the black top, landing on his hands. I sprang onto his back, and held him loosely, hoping he would try to stand. When he raised his leg and planted his foot, I leaned across his back and slipped my leg between his, hooking his raised leg with my foot.

I grabbed his other leg with both hands, pulled his knee behind my head and arched my back. He fell backwards on top of me, but that was okay, I had my hold.

My arching pulled his legs apart and I heard the muscles in his groin and lower back pop, doubtless tearing as they stretched.

The "banana splits" had been a nasty wrestling move before they outlawed it. The drawbacks were, it left your opponent's hands free to punch with, and it was not a good pinning hold, but when applied properly it was painful, even dangerous. I learned it while wrestling in high school. I was never the best but I was far from the worst!

As Wilson began to breathe murderous threats, it dawned on me that kissing and making up wasn't in the cards, so I wrenched harder.

Within moments a crowd of Master-at-Arms, and transients surrounded Wilson and I, and rather than breaking us up they began taking odds, all in Wilson's favor.

I loosened my hold slightly, hoping he would appreciate my mercy and show some gratitude, but instead he punched me in the nose, the crowd went wild. The taste of my own blood infuriated me and I arched my back as hard as I could. He began to groan and beg.

"Uncle?" I suggested, as whimsically as I could make myself sound under the circumstances.

"Uncle, uncle, uncle!" he shouted.

"Uncle who?" Cruelty wasn't my nature, but I was still tasting blood.

"Uncle Squirrel, uncle Squirrel!"

"Wrong answer!" I wrenched again with all my strength, and held it.

He screamed and writhed in agony laced with anger, "I don't know your fucking name!"

"You harass me daily and don't know my fucking name? Well you'd better find out what it is!" I knew from the sound of his voice that freeing him while he could still walk, or kick would be a serious mistake.

Someone in the crowd asked, "Does anyone know what the squirrel's name is?" No one seemed to know.

20

Wilson mustered a desperate swing at my face, which I blocked. In turn I released a series of punches with my free hand to his well exposed groin, and afterward I knew he was done.

A sailor returning from the personnel office shouted, "Sam—his name is Sam."

"Uncle Sam, Uncle Sam," Wilson screamed.

"That wasn't so hard now, was it?" I untangled myself from Wilson and rose to my feet. Leaving him sprawling in pain on the blacktop I pushed my way through the spellbound crowd. I knew it would be several days before Wilson could walk properly, let alone kick, and I was pretty sure he wouldn't kick me again.

Chapter Five

O longapo, the city outside the gates of the Subic Bay Naval Station was known worldwide for its nightlife, nightclubs, beautiful women and world class musicians. In 1975 there were approximately one hundred, fifty thousand registered bar girls working in the local bars, and an estimated one hundred thousand unregistered. Some of the girls had been products of white slavery, but most of them came from poor families in the southern provinces, looking for prosperity.

Contrary to popular thinking, Olongapo did not represent the culture of the Philippines. Beyond Olongapo, holding hands with a girl prior to marriage was considered taboo, and to their discredit most American servicemen did not realize this.

The bar girls had a saying, "Lahat ng marine ay gagoo!" (All marines are crazy!). Expecting marines to be sane after being cooped up on a ship for months, and enduring the Marine's style of discipline is like shaking a warm bottle of soda pop and expecting it not to spray. Sailors were crazy too, but not crazy enough to merit a saying.

Over a period of three weeks the bodies of three marines were found beheaded in East Bajac Bajac.

Posted near the gates were warnings in both English and Tagalog that East Bajac Bajac was off-limits to military personnel.

I had nothing to worry about in the earlier part of my tour, I kept to the base, and refrained from drinking. In my free time I busied myself with courses in mechanics and Tagalog, in which I excelled.

As time wore on, the arduous duty, and military bullshit took its toll, and although I practiced moderation I found myself spending more time in Olongapo. My life was best described in the words of a Simon and Garfunkel song, "there were times when I felt so lonesome I took some comfort there."

I read komiks (Philippine comic books), in order to pick up the slang because few of the locals spoke correct Tagalog. Occasionally I practiced conversation, but only with select Filipino friends because it served me better to listen. I discovered from listening that the women thought I was attractive, and the men thought I was stupid. The "Stupid" part occasionally prompted me to respond in Tagalog. Not to refute that I was stupid, but by simply joining in the conversation I brought shock and embarrassment to those who badmouthed me.

The Acme Club, located just outside the gate on the third floor of a three story building became my favorite hangout. The band was incredibly talented, imitating Led Zeplin and other great bands with a high level of accuracy.

The women, hostesses and go-go dancers alike, knew that I was only there for the beer and music, and they left me alone.

It came as a surprise one night when a very attractive young woman sat down beside me and asked my name. Assuming she was a new hostess who wanted me to buy her a drink, for which she would receive a commission, I responded, "I don't buy ladies drinks!"

She blinked, seemingly offended, but responded kindly with, "I don't work here, and I have my own money. How about if I buy you a drink?"

I couldn't turn it down, and what was to be one drink turned into several one mores. When I told her I could drink no more, she asked if I would like to go to her place.

I was thinking "no," when I heard myself say "yes," at least that's the way I recall it.

I followed her down the steps to the bustling streets of Olongapo, where she flagged down a "Special Jeepney," (one that doesn't make the prescribed route, but can be hired as a taxi). We got out of the jeepney in a poorly lighted area where two-story buildings bordered a dark city street with intersecting blind alleyways. After the jeepney drove away, we stood together in the quiet.

"Wait here, I'll be right back," she said.

With an about face, she ran off down an alley where she turned again and seemingly vanished among the structures.

My ears attuned to the sound of mumbling across the street, as five shadowy figures walked my direction. I looked to my right, and observed another small crowd of men coming toward me. From my left—seven or eight more were headed toward me. Within moments I was surrounded, and as more joined, pressing in around me, any notion of escape seemed unthinkable.

A stocky man, thirtyish, about five foot, nine, forced his way through the crowd. When he reached me he leaned his shoulder against my chest, and pulled a cigarette from an opened pack in his shirt pocket. Placing the cigarette in his mouth he muttered, "You gotta match, Joe?"

It dawned on me that I was in East Bajac Bajac, where the marines had been beheaded. The girl had set me up, and these men were not wellwishers intending to see me safely back to the base.

"Walla akong fosboro!" (I have no matches) I said, adding, "Ayokong cigeralio!" (I don't like cigarettes).

The stocky fellow pulled the cigarette from his mouth. "You speak our language!"

The crowd, my would-be assailants, began to chatter among themselves, and all at once I found myself overwhelmed with a myriad of questions in Tagalog which could not be answered in a moment or even an hour.

They took me to a Sari Sari store (a little bit of everything store). We sat on benches outside the small building where the gang bought me beer and pancit until I could eat and drink no more. I gave them only my middle name, "Joel," but they called me "Kabayan," (fellow countryman). None of them had ever heard an American speak their language, and they were fully entertained by my stories and jokes, and my "bigkus" or accent.

When the midnight curfew had given way to the wee morning hours, they offered to escort me back to the base. They told me not to worry about the Philippine Constabulary, who, during the martial law of that time, were likened to the Nazi S.S., and had gone so far as to kill Americans caught out after curfew.

The Constabulary seemed to know my new-found fellow countrymen who walked me back to the base, and at every checkpoint the constabulary waved us on, and I, thanks to my assailants turned friends, strode without a care, like a cat with more than nine lives crossing a busy freeway.

The curfew was not enforced on the base where military personnel worked around the clock.

Each night at midnight the computer center printed the base readout, a classified list of ships and personnel, both transient, and permanent along with their various locations, and phone numbers. On my duty nights I was charged with picking up the readouts and delivering them to all the commands around the Subic Bay Naval Station as well as the hospital and the neighboring Naval Air Station at Cubi Point.

I was provided a different Master-at-Arms truck each night for making the deliveries. Sometimes the trucks were equipped with police radios, police lights and sirens. Sometimes they were bare-bone pickups, although all of them were navy grey, drawn from the Fleet Motor-pool of sixty-seven Chevys or seventy-one Fords. I was seldom given the same truck twice. After picking up the readouts I dropped copies at the Brigg, Armed Forces Police Station and various other commands before turning onto the mountainous jungle road that led to the hospital.

During daylight hours the road to the hospital offered a scenic view of massive trees adorned with hanging vines and jungle foliage, alive with exotic creatures, colorful birds, and monkeys. At night cobras and pythons were the only wildlife, but I enjoyed the drive nonetheless, it enabled me to escape the confines of Receiving Station.

On one occasion I was halfway thru the jungle when an All-PointsBulletin came over the radio, **"All units be on the lookout for an Armed**

Forces Police truck, stolen from the Brigg at twelve fifteen A.M."

I chuckled and muttered, "What kind of idiot would steal an Armed Forces Police truck?" *I had just dropped a readout at the Brigg. Did I see anything suspicious? Not to my knowledge.* "Ohmygosh!" I gasped, as reality began to set in. I couldn't recall my truck having a police radio.

As the dispatcher read the numbers to the stolen truck I followed those same numbers stenciled on the dash in front of me. I was driving the stolen truck!

Panic stricken, I searched my mind for a solution.

Honesty was always the best policy. I could simply return the truck and explain that my key had started the wrong vehicle, (a flaw common to sixty-seven Chevys), and that it was parked right next to mine. Of course they would take into consideration my sleep deprivation, and the fact that the trucks all looked alike. Surely they would simply accept my apology and laugh the matter off.

BULLSHIT! They would hang my scurvy ass from the yard arms!

I pulled the truck over to the side of the road about a mile from the hospital. Removing my shirt I carefully wiped down the steering wheel and shifter, and anything else I might have touched, as well as the door handles.

Taking the readouts in hand, I sprinted on foot the remaining mile through the jungle. After dropping a readout at the hospital I caught a taxi back to the Brigg where I retrieved the duty vehicle and finished my route.

The following day I was surprised to learn that the incident had made the base newspaper. One of my co-workers remarked, "What kind of idiot would steal an Armed Forces Police truck and abandon it in the jungle?" I could only smile and agree with him.

Chapter Six

"**W**ould you like a menu?" the waitress, a nice looking young
lady with a red checkered apron asked.

"No thanks, but I'll have a Coke, please." I was anxious
to get back to the conversation.

Shellie sipped her Coke and leaned forward. "I hope you don't mind, I
ordered my Coke before you came."

"Not at all," I said, wondering at my own mixed feelings. Gone were
her youth and beauty, and yet I was consumed with the kind of joy I
would expect to feel at the sight of my oldest, dearest friend after a long
absence.

Her face had broadened, and taken on a wrinkle here, a sag there.
Traces of the girl I once knew still remained, although few. Years of
sadness and joy had left their lines and marks, and I wondered which
contributed most—joy I hoped. Her smile had changed little, and it
awakened in me memories of the happiness I felt when I gazed upon it
long ago.

Her eyes seemed to scan my face the way my mother used to look me
over before a church service, ready to lick her hand and paste down all my
wild hair.

"Is something wrong?" I asked.

"No, I just can't get over how good you look, and how good it is to
see you." Her voice slipped from alto to a slightly higher pitch in mid-
sentence, it was something she did when she was happy and meant what
she said. She was never one to hide her feelings—I liked that about her.

Nestling slightly in her seat, like a child anxious to hear a fairytale she
continued, "So tell me more about the Philippines. What was it like?" She
took a sip from her straw, and gave me that ice-cold Coke held back by a
puckered smile look.

Sam Welch

I stifled the urge to laugh as I raised my right hand and made a slow sweeping motion. "The lightening in the Philippines during the rainy season starts at one end of the horizon and travels clear across the night sky. It's usually followed by unbelievable torrents of rain. The next morning mushrooms sprout up everywhere. It's like a different world, strange and beautiful. In the countryside—dirt roads separate the rice fields, and during my morning walks in the barrio, little children followed me, some of them naked, just to catch a glimpse at an American. More joined with each thatched hut I passed until they became a chattering crowd. When I turned they disbursed quickly, hiding behind clumps of grass, or each other."

I drew a breath, cleared and continued, "Banana trees grow wild along with guavas and mangos, and vendors carry boxes of rice bread, known as pandisal, and the banana bread is the best I've ever eaten."

"Mmmmm, that sounds so good."

"Yes it does," I agreed, "I'm making myself hungry. Enough about me—you haven't told me anything about yourself."

"My life is mundane. Please tell me more."

I didn't want to talk about my navy years, I wanted a two way conversation, a give and take chat, and although I found myself giving more than taking, my stories seemed to make her happy, and in that I found some contentment.

*

The quality of life at Receiving Station changed for the better when the last of the refugees were processed, and the personnel who were on loan returned.

I advanced in rank from E-2 to E-3, which gave me a few more dollars to spend.

The old Lieutenant retired, and a much kinder man, a lieutenant commander, replaced him.

28

The Chief Master at Arms retired as well, and a new master chief, a black man by the name of Tate, one of the finest men I've ever met, took his place.

Within a matter of weeks life at RecSta took a one hundred eighty degree turn for the better, reminding me of the song about Camp Granada.

Duty at RecSta went from almost intolerable to an eight hour day— five days a week with one twenty-four hour additional shift every seventh day. The icing covered the cake when the no-load petty officer who delegated all of his work to me transferred and was replaced by a petty officer who pulled his own weight.

Overwhelmed by all the free time that a regular work week gave me, I decided to ride a Victory Liner bus to Manila on a Saturday.

The Victory Liner was the Greyhound of the Philippines, although the culture and customs of the Philippines made traveling much different than traveling in America.

The roads were poorly maintained, sometimes treacherous. During the monsoon season entire stretches of highway washed away. Traffic laws, all unwritten, were simple and easy to follow. Larger vehicles always had the right-of-way. Jeepneys and the common tricycle, (a motorcycle with a covered sidecar) were required to yield to larger trucks and busses or they were promptly ran off the road. Pedestrians crossed at their own risk, and fatalities among those who dared defy the rules of the road were common.

Busses ranged in luxury along with cost of fare. Wealthier passengers could opt for the more lavish "Deluxe" coach with plush seats and air conditioning, while the majority of the Filipinos settled for hard seats and open windows. I felt uncomfortable living beyond the means of the average Filipino. I wanted to experience the life of an ordinary person, not some candy-coated fallacy, and so I rode the standard coach.

The busses were often crowded with latecomers forced to stand in the aisle. Some travelers carried sundry foods or livestock such as chickens, small pigs and goats. During the frequent stops the coach filled with unfiltered cigarette smoke, diesel fumes, animal odors, and the smell of human perspiration. Relief came only when the bus reached cruising speeds and the sweltering wind purged the coach. Even the Filipinos who were accustomed to such travel often remarked, "Sarap ng hangin" (the wind is delicious).

The bus passed over the mountains of Bataan, reaching speeds upwards of seventy miles per hour on the straightaways and braking suddenly for the switchback turns. After an hour of hairpin curves the road straightened and flattened into miles of lovely fertile banana groves and rice fields tilled by Filipinos wearing platter shaped woven hats, plowing with water buffalo.

When the bus made scheduled stops vendors flocked under the windows selling bananas, corn on the cob, coconuts with straws, soft drinks, and the ever popular balut (a partially incubated duck egg). Balut was a delicacy among the nationals. They opened the balut by tapping it on the frame of the seat in front of them. Once the balut was opened they slurped the colloidal, blood vessel strewn embryo from the shell with great vigor.

I was offered balut by good intentioned Filipinos who claimed it was delicious, nutritious, and an aphrodisiac! I told them I would rather starve and go impotent, and I remain convinced that if balut had been the fruit on the tree of knowledge of good and evil, we'd probably still be in the Garden of Eden, because Adam and Eve wouldn't have touched it.

I got off the bus in Cubao, a suburb of Manila. The streets were dirty and smelled of raw sewage from Japanese style benjo ditches which ran beneath the sidewalks. Smog from busses, cars, burning garbage, and firewood over which street vendors cooked, filled the already balmy, late morning air. I strolled along the city streets browsing through shops and malls.

Around midday I stepped into a Chinese restaurant, and ordered Pansit Canton. When it arrived it neither tasted nor smelled like the pansit I was used to, but because of my hunger I ate without complaint.

By mid-afternoon I was feeling sick and nauseated, and I decided to return to the Victory Liner Station.

At the ticket sales window I learned that because of the curfew there were only a few more busses returning to Olongapo that afternoon. I waited patiently in line as hundreds of Filipinos crowded in front of me, pushing and shoving to board two of the busses. When the third bus began boarding, I managed, despite my weakened state, to force my way through the crowd. Finding a seat halfway back along the aisle, I painfully sat down.

Passengers desperate to reach Olongapo before curfew continued to crowd in filling the aisles.

Smoke from the harsh native cigarettes and animal odors from chickens, ducks, small pigs and goats filled the air adding to my nausea, and causing me to wonder how the rest of the passengers could even breathe.

The crowd that stood in the aisle swayed and staggered to the sudden starts, stops, and turns as the bus got underway, most of them had little to brace themselves on.

I remained as still as possible while the bus travelled over the flat lands between Manila and Bataan, although my stomach had begun to cramp and my nausea worsened. The monotonous hum of the engine was interrupted only by the rhythmic clack as the bus crossed the seams of the concrete road, and the occasional horn blast warning jeepneys and tricycles to move or face the consequences.

An elderly woman in the seat beside me took notice of my condition, and when the bus stopped she insisted that coconut milk would make me feel better.

I bought a large coconut with a straw in it, and at the woman's insistence, forced down the fluid. The coconut milk made me sicker, and when the bus reached the mountains of Bataan, with its winding roads and sharp switchback turns—I, unable to control myself, wretched violently into the aisle.

31

Sam Welch

The colloidal vomit spread up and down the aisle with the bus's sudden braking and acceleration, making the rigid rubber slicker than ice, and creating a hazardous condition for the fifty or so passengers standing in it. The driver, who was on a deadline, could not slow down, and the standing passengers fell like dominos, only to recover and fall again as the bus braked for the hairpin curves. After repeated attempts to stand some of the passengers decided to remain where they had fallen, piled on top of each other but even then they continued to slide back and forth on the slippery surface.

Cackling chickens flew overhead, feathers fluttered about the coach, squealing pigs scampered over the fallen passengers. I overheard Filipinos cursing me as well as the day that MacArthur returned.

When the bus reached Olongapo I got off and distanced myself quickly from the disgruntled passengers and hurried back to the base.

*

"Would you care for a refill?" The waitress was back.

Shellie swirled the Coke in her glass, visibly dismayed by the content of my story as she stared at her glass. It was less than half full. She seemed to recover quickly with, "Sure, why not?"

The waitress cast me that oh-so-cute smile that women only give men when they're with another woman. I never figured out what it meant, only that it was a woman thing.

I smiled back. "I've still got plenty, thank you."

Shellie handed her glass to the waitress. If she noticed the flirtation, she never let on, and as the waitress turned to leave, Shellie addressed me with that all-knowing, penetrating, *I'll know if you lie to me* smile and asked,
"were you able to stay out of trouble all that time?"

"How did I know that was coming?" I took a sip of Coke, the glass was too small to hide behind, and the weight of her gaze seemed to pierce

32

my defenses. I never could lie to her. I simply had to think of some coy way to sidestep the question.

I lowered the glass and tilted it as if to point at her, and with a mild French accent said, "Madam, you have me confused with someone else."

"Your alter ego, no doubt, Dr. Jeckyl."

"Now wait a minute, I've always been well intentioned," I defended, "I just have a knack for being in the wrong place at the wrong time."

The waitress was back with the Coke." Shellie thanked her, but not before giving her that one-eyebrow-raised, *you're not putting anything over on me* look.

The waitress followed with "You're welcome," avoiding Shellie's gaze as she turned abruptly and walked away.

"What was that all about?" I said knowing I'd just nailed the opportunity to change the subject.

"Whatever do you mean?"

Shellie's question was so innocent that I knew better than to pursue the matter although it wreaked of, *if you pursue this I'll deny it and you'll look ridiculous!* It was indeed a girl thing, *guys* were not allowed to understand, and I had to leave it at that.

She took another sip, a tiny sip that meant she wanted to hear the whole story before the Coke ran out. "Now where were we?"

"The beauty of the Philippines." I waved my hand slowly in front of me. "The lightening as it crosses the horizon at night. Banana trees…"

"No, you covered that already. Hmm, seems like there was something I was going to ask, but it must not have been that important."

"I never got in any trouble." I held my face perfectly straight and gazed directly into her eyes. It was the honest truth, and although there were a few close calls, a miss is as good as a mile!

*

In 1976 Olongapo adapted a city ordinance. Philippine women were no longer allowed to walk with American Servicemen on the two main streets, Rizal Avenue and Magsaysay Boulevard without walking papers. The papers could be purchased from the city for around five dollars. There was supposed to be a one week grace period before the law was enforced.

I had little to worry about, I seldom walked with girls, but there was that one exception; Alice was her name, and I could almost see her face in my mind. She wasn't my girlfriend, although I hung out with her sometimes. Alice was beautiful, and she loved me, but she was bad to the bone, and I didn't love her. Ah, maybe I did, like a bad habit! She had skills, they included karate. She nailed me once with a roundhouse that even Wilson would have applauded, leaving me floored, but grateful that she wasn't wearing high heels.

We knew better than to walk together on Magsaysay so she walked a little ahead of me, but she made the mistake of turning to speak to me.

Three Filipino men bolted onto the sidewalk from the curb and grabbed her. I thought we were being robbed, and I struck the closest one in the face with all my strength. He went down fast and hard. The other two released her and came at me. I dropped them as well. Several more men rushed to subdue me, all at separate intervals, giving me time to recoil. They fell one after the next. I glanced at what I had done in utter disbelief, they were laying all over the place. Suddenly I felt the unmistakable impression of cold steel against the back of my head and heard that distinctive metallic click that can only mean one thing. I half-turned just enough to see one of the men holding a Smith thirty-eight. The hammer was back, his nose was bleeding, his hand quivering.

I raised my hands slowly, "Okay, you can have her," I blurted.

Faster than my life could flash before my eyes, and less than a block away the squealing tires of a U.S. Armed Forces Police paddy-wagon left a patch of rubber and a small smoke cloud in its wake. Lights and siren clashed with the sound of Olongapo's night life, as the vehicle sped toward me. An Armed Forces Police Officer sprang from the running board, while the truck was still rolling, and crossed the sidewalk shouting, "It's okay, we'll take him from here!" He continued to calm the gunman with words like, "We got him. He's our jurisdiction!"

The cop cuffed me and locked me in the back of the paddy-wagon. They took me back to the Armed Forces Police Station on the base where they removed the cuffs and released me. I tried to explain what had happened, but they had seen the whole thing, and needed no explanation. Evidently the gunman and the other assailants were plain clothed, under cover, Philippine Constabulary.

"You're free to go," the cop told me, adding, "You don't realize how close you came to getting your head blown off, so I wouldn't go back out there tonight if I were you."

I asked him if he had ever heard the Philippine phrase, "mag kamukha kayong lahat?"

He shook his head "no."

I told him, "Filipinos use it when speaking of Americans. It means 'you all look alike to me'. We all look alike to them!" I added.

I returned to my barracks, where I changed to a different color of shirt, dawned a baseball cap, and went back out on the town. The following day I bailed Alice out of jail.

*

"So you kept your nose clean," Shellie's statement was more like a question, and more than a bit facetious. "I'm proud of you." She nodded and continued with, "You married in the Philippines. How did you meet your wife?"

"I met her at a Beach Resort, she was home from college…"

*

White Rock Resort had a huge swimming pool surrounded by a broad meandering walkway with umbrella covered tables and chairs. There was a bar at one end of the pool with a thatched grass roof, where all kinds of drinks and refreshments were served to those who could not wait for the roving waiters and waitresses. The resort also offered rental cabins along a white sandy beach strewn about with coconut palms that cast shade on the crystal blue surf. Admission to the pool was cheap, and the location between Olongapo and Subic made it the perfect Saturday afternoon get-away.

White Rock was not the sort of place to take a girl out for a date. There was never a shortage of attractive, single women. They weren't snooty, nor did they play hard to get like the women back home. If they liked a guy or found him attractive they told him.

For a while advances from beautiful women served a therapeutic purpose in restoring my damaged self-esteem, but after a while it grew old.

I found myself longing to meet a girl who didn't need to impress me.

They say the way to a man's heart is through his stomach. For me that was partly true, but my fetish had nothing to do with food—it was beer. I never turned one down, and women often bought me beer.

Maybe it was the pollen in the air that day, the moon or the alignment of the planets, pheromones, or some weird shit, or maybe a window had opened; a window that only opens once in a young man's life when he meets that special girl.

"Are you the girl who offered to buy me a beer?" I asked, as I stood over the table where she was seated. I had one hand raised above my brow to shield my eyes from the sun.

"I'm certain I don't know what you're talking about," she replied in perfect English, as though I had just offered her the strangest pick-up line she had ever heard. Her hair was well kept, jet black, shoulder length. She wore no makeup, her face, lovely as well, needed none.

I glanced about at the surrounding tables, it had come down to a process of elimination. Attractive, black hair, brown eyed, well-tanned, bikini clad Filipino women were everywhere, and I was never one for recalling or differentiating between bathing suit colors or designs.

Feeling a little out of place, I decided to explain myself, "I was on the other side of the pool when a young lady said that if I came over to

36

this table, she would buy me a beer. That was about ten minutes ago. I told her I would come over as soon as I finished the beer that I was drinking. I finished that beer, and here I am!"

"Well it wasn't me. I don't know anything about it, and I am not going to buy you a beer." She blinked a few times, shook her head, and cast me a bewildered half-smile.

I didn't mean to be intrusive, but a beer was at stake here! "One last question," I persisted, "and I'll leave you alone; is there another young lady who was sitting at this table with you, or are you by yourself?"

"My cousin was here earlier. I don't know where she went. She'll probably be back soon. If you'd like, you can wait for her. Maybe she's the one you're looking for."

"In that case, do you mind if I sit down?"

"Go ahead." She motioned at the chair in front of me.

As I sat down, she took a pack of cigarettes from the center of the table. Pulling one out, she put it in her mouth. "Would you care for a cigarette?" she asked.

"No thank you, I don't smoke."

Removing the cigarette from her lips, she set it on the table and said, "Neither do I."

I felt a smile form on my face, and I fought hard to keep it at a mere smile. I couldn't pin-point exactly what it was that entranced me most about that moment, and yet I'm sure it would take volumes to explain—it was the kind of overwhelming, inexplicable facet in time that leaves an orator at a loss for words, and a writer impotent, and out of ink. As if the code words that had been programed into my mind from some preconceived era had just been spoken over a pack of cigarettes. I knew she was the one!

"I'm going to marry you," I mumbled, then added, "Oh look, is that your cousin?" I pointed behind her to a young woman coming from the bar with a beer and two cocktails in her hands. She was looking directly at us, and I knew my rescue, in more than one sense, was on the way.

Sam Welch

The sweat on the ice-cold bottle, even from a distance, made my mouth water, and helped to take the heat off.

She glanced around, "Yes, that's my cousin, Ning," turning back, she continued, "but it sounded like you said…"

"I did say that. I'm going to marry you," I repeated as Ning approached the table.

"Ning, this is…" She motioned and turned to me, pausing in midsentence. "I'm sorry, I didn't get your name."

"Sam." I stood up to greet Ning, and accept my beer.

"Sam is waiting here for a beer, and he thinks he's going to marry me!"

"Hi Ning, thanks for the beer," I said.

"Yes, I met Sam." Glancing at me, Ning continued, "You probably say that to all the girls, don't you Sam?"

"Would you believe me if I say, no?" I raised the beer to my mouth and took a sip, the cool flavor refreshed me, and the bottle seemed almost big enough to hide behind.

Ning smiled and shook her head. "No, you're right I don't."

"And your name is?" I turned to the young lady across the table.

Ning cut in with a chuckle, "you mean you haven't even met Carmen and you've already proposed?"

"Carmen," she extended her hand sheepishly.

"Pleased to meet you Carmen." I shook her hand gently, acting as nonchalant as possible, knowing that my strange behavior would be accepted as normal for a foreigner regardless of whether she believed me, as long as I acted confident.

"Pleased to meet you too." Her face lacked enthusiasm, but I expected no less under the circumstances. If a strange woman had told me she was going to marry me, I would have drank it off, slept it off and laughed it off all at her expense, and then locked my door and forgotten her name.

Carmen, on the other hand, was more accepting than I, and what began as a strange first meeting turned into a mutual lifetime commitment.

*

Shellie took another sip of her Coke. "Sounds like a match made in Heaven, and you've been married what—seventeen years now?"

"Yes, and overall it's been good, and I think she would say the same."

"That's wonderful, so tell me more," she beamed with an expression of genuine interest.

Not wanting to disappoint her, but feeling as though the conversation was lop-sided in my favor I said, "I'm doing all the talking. I've yet to hear a single thing about you."

"Well." She rolled her eyes upward as if in remembrance. "I saw you in Hanscam's Market in eighty-one."

"You saw me, and you didn't say anything? You should have at least said hello."

"You were busy, and I was pregnant with my second daughter."

"You have two daughters?"

She nodded "yes," and forced a half-smile.

"I'll bet they're both brilliant and witty!" I couldn't help but chuckle, as I pictured Shellie in her younger days, and I imagined her daughters were much like her. I glanced into her eyes, her enjoyment seemed to be fading.

"And how are Joan and Henry?"

"Mom's on her back again, and Dad retired. He still fishes when he's not looking after Mom."

"On her back?" The phrase was familiar, but I couldn't recall what it meant. It seemed like something I hadn't heard for nineteen years.

"Mom has back problems. That means she's on the couch."

"Oh yeah, I had forgotten, sorry to hear that. Tell her I said to get well soon."

39

Shellie took another small sip. Her smile returned. "Please tell me more."

She seemed more than a little anxious to hear my story, and so I began, "You have to realize that somewhere between the 'once upon a time' and the 'happily ever after' something always goes terribly amiss!"

Her eyes widened and I knew her interest had deepened. I had no fairytales to offer I drew a deep saddened breath and began a story that I didn't want to tell.

Chapter Seven

C armen and I married in July of 1976, and I was transferred in September to Coronado, California for BUD/S training (Basic Underwater Demolition/Navy Seal Training). We exchanged tearful goodbyes at Clark Air Force Base near Angeles City, Philippines, not knowing when we would see each other again or that we were expecting our first child.

I didn't go into BUD/S because I wanted to be a tough Navy Seal or wear the prestigious Trident insignia, I went because I needed more money. My allotments for house payments kept me financially drained, and the training would afford me an additional $55 per month hazardous duty pay.
After training hazardous duty pay would increase to $110 a month.

The rigors of BUD/S proved a rude awakening from the peaceful life to which I had become accustomed, but I was strong and more agile than most.

Around two-hundred young men began the training, but by the end of the first week only forty-eight remained in the class. Most of the men dropped out during or after a long ocean swim against the current in forty-seven degree water. We were not allowed to wear fins or wetsuits during that swim and a large percentage of the dropouts failed because they seized up from hypothermia and had to be rescued. After the first long swim those of us who remained in the training were issued fins but wetsuits were not allowed.

Every practical training exercise, or "evolution," was preceded by a class. At the end of every class we were given a test that rivalled any college level exam. During the six months of training, "tadpoles," as we were known were allowed to fail two evolutions. This rule was overlooked and waived for critical ratings such as Hospital Corpsmen, because they were badly needed in the teams. For men in less critical ratings it was strictly enforced. None of the instructors had ever seen a Personnelman, (admin type) such as myself in BUD/S, and no one knew what to think of it.

Since the Viet Nam War had ended, fewer billets were available in the teams. President Carter, who had just taken office, wanted cut-backs wherever they could be found, and one rumor had it that the BUD/S command planned to weed out enough men to make it feasible to combine two of the three annual classes for the diving phase of training.

The instructors joked that training had become tougher than it was during war-time when it was shortened to two phases, and the objective had turned from passing as many as possible to eliminating as many as possible. This was done by making the training so torturous that most tadpoles quit amid ridicule and humiliation from the instructors.

Although quitting was considered a shameful act, it was as simple as ringing the brass bell outside the BUD/S command building and calling out, "I quit, I quit, I quit!" Occasionally Tadpoles suffered debilitating injuries that prevented them from continuing. Most of the injured men were extremely relieved to find an honorable way out. Others who wanted to continue, despite some disability, were simply set back to the next class and given a second chance. The setback procedure was also adhered to in cases other than injuries, although each case was judged individually.

An evolution known as drown-proofing reduced the class considerably. Our hands and feet were tied behind our backs, and we were required to wriggle across the huge base pool. This evolution separated negative buoyancy tadpoles from those who were positive buoyancy, in short, those who sink from those who float. Since most of the black tadpoles were negative buoyancy they had a hard time passing this evolution while the majority of the white tadpoles, who were positive buoyancy, found it easier to pass. I, being that one in a thousand white men who is extremely negative buoyancy, succeeded by biting my tee-shirt before they tied my hands. Once in the water, I blew air into the shirt to use it as a floatation device while I bobbed and wriggled.

Another evolution that targeted negative buoyancy tadpoles was the practical life-saving exam. I was among those who failed, but because it was my only failure, I was allowed to continue in the training.

We were required to swim out in the deep end of the pool and rescue the instructors who were anything but passive, and very unwilling to be rescued.

In the classroom prior to the practical evolution, we were told that if the instructor who was being rescued sensed any inadequacies in the rescue swimmer's ability to keep the instructor's head above water the instructor would turn on the swimmer.

When one of the senior chiefs offered to test some of us on the side of the pool where the water was only six feet deep, I fell in line not realizing that the deeper water was to my advantage. When it came my turn I dove in and correctly performed the arm drag, chin tilt, and cross chest carry.

The Senior Chief, who was six foot, five, and well over two-hundred pounds, turned on me, locking his legs around my chest, and holding me underwater. I was unable to surface or break free, and although I tried to take him down to the bottom, hoping he would release me and go for air, I could not go deep enough to take his head underwater.

I struggled in vain to free myself from his scissor hold. When I passed out, he pulled me by my limp arm to the surface where I revived, but even then I had no strength.

"Are you ready to go again, 'cuz I'm about to put your shit-bird ass back underwater?"

"No please, Senior Chief," I heard myself say.

He looked around at the instructors on the side of the pool. It seemed he had everyone's attention. "Did you hear that? Isn't that sweet? No, please Senior Chief," he mimicked in a mousy voice, adding, "he just begged me not to put him back underwater!" With a shove, he forced me toward the edge of the pool. "Now get the fuck out of my pool shit-bird, and why don't you go ring the bell while you're at it!"

Amid the laughter from instructors and fellow tadpoles alike I pulled myself from the pool never having felt so physically drained or humiliated. I determined that I would not ring the bell, and that I would die rather than beg for my life again.

*

P.T., or physical training was rigorous, beginning at five A.M. on the grinder in the BUD/S compound. One instructor led the class, while others watched to make sure the tadpoles performed the exercises properly.

Between exercises we were required to sing. If we didn't come up with a song the entire class was punished in some creative fashion. Sometimes we were all required to run to the ocean and drench ourselves in the surf, sometimes we all lined up and hit the tub one after another.

The tub was an old claw-foot bathtub filled with water, usually reserved for those who couldn't keep their backs straight during push-ups, or their legs straight during flutter kicks. Offenders were required to immerse themselves totally and then hustle back to their place in P.T. formation. Occasionally the instructors added bags of crushed ice to the water to make the experience more entertaining for them.

"Hitting the tub," as it was called, in the morning made an already promised bad day—worse. We didn't have time to change, and it took half a day to dry out.

Repeat offenders, and those who couldn't make the required time on the timed runs were assigned to the "circus," a torturous, end of the week—workout-till-you-drop-from-physical-punishment session, or until the instructors grew tired of abusing you, which wasn't likely.

On one occasion I ended up in the circus. Not because of poor performance on a timed run, or bent legged flutter kicks, but because a Warrant Officer caught me hiding behind a storage pod taking pictures of the circus.

My reason for taking pictures, although it seemed stupid in retrospect, was in response to a letter from my mother, who could not understand why the men in my military training class were performing in a circus. I intended to send her a picture and thereby save a thousand words.

The instructors took my camera and used up the film, some of it on me as I played along with their torturous games. After having it developed, they posted some of the pictures on the command billboard. Weeks later they returned the camera along with a few of the pictures.

The obstacle course, or "O course" as it was known, was interesting and even fun. It served as a relief from the long runs in soft sand, long cold ocean swims, and grueling classroom. The "O course," like all good obstacle courses, included a wall, a net climb, a slide for life, and numerous other obstacles that required sliding hand-over-hand down ropes, and weaving over and under logs.

The tower was perhaps the toughest most frightening obstacle, although after a couple of weeks of running the O-course daily, I found myself looking forward to it. The tower was a three story log building without walls or stairs, it could only be scaled by hurling one's self, leg-first from story to story from the outside, and pulling the body up and over each floor.

We left the start line one at a time, at stop-watch intervals to keep from overrunning each other. Instructors gave us the "go" signal, and recorded our time.

The third week of training was known as "Hell Week," an entire week without sleep.

Instructors burst into the barracks on a Saturday night firing automatic weapons (with blank rounds), and screaming, above the continuous gun blasts, "Get out!"

I rushed into the hallway, dressing as I ran through the smoke-filled air. The tadpoles ahead of me were sliding and falling on the tens of thousands of spent blank rounds that covered the floor and rolled beneath their feet.

45

Once outside the barracks, we were told to form up on the grinder (the blacktop inside the BUD/S compound).

At one end of the grinder were six fully inflated large black rubber rafts known as I.B.S. boats (Inflatable Boat Small). Each boat had eight paddles.

We were divided into six boat crews, eight men to a crew. Each crew of eight was assigned a boat. The boats were carried overhead at a jog with arms extended.

The class became smaller with each tadpole that dropped out, leaving fewer men to carry a boat that grew heavier each day because of fatigue. Some of the boat crews became so small that the men had to be reassigned creating boat crews of mixed height. Taller men carried more than their share of a boat that bounced and hammered them with every stride, while shorter men couldn't reach the boat.

We carried the boats constantly except during timed runs, O-course, long ocean swims, and ocean excursions where we paddled the boats. We practiced launching through the surf and coming in again. That night the waves were moderate, and the instructors entertained themselves, watching us get dumped and pounded by the waves.

The most dangerous evolution involving the I.B.S. boats was "Rock Portage," landing, launching, and carrying the boats over a rock jetty. More than one tadpole suffered broken bones during the exercise.

Wednesday of Hell Week, was a clear cold November day, our fourth day without sleep. We paddled south of Coronado to the mud flats where we crawled around in a network of muddy canals performing one pointless exercise after another. When nighttime rolled around we were provided ponchos which could be converted into small two man pup tents. After pitching the tents we were told we would be allowed to sleep, and for mere seconds at a time we were allowed to share precious body warmth as we shivered in the near freezing night air wearing only drenched tee shirts and fatigues.

One man at a time was required to remain on watch duty. The watch had to be relieved every two minutes, and the watchman, who was given a stopwatch, had to shout the correct time every thirty seconds followed by the words, "and all is well in beautiful camp swampy!"

Each time someone messed up, and mess-ups were frequent, we were ordered to dive into the nearest muddy canal, and bring up a bottom sample in our chattering teeth before running back to our tents where sleep was impossible.

The class was a little smaller by morning, and our young ensign, the only remaining officer was instructed to lead us in P.T. Steam rose from his wet tee-shirt in the early morning sun, as he attempted to bark out orders with his hoarse voice, mustering little more than a whisper.

After P.T. the instructors had us lash the boats together upside down to form a bridge across one of the canals. Our teetering bridge of I.B.S. boats became a playing field for a shoving match that pitted one boat crew against another. The boat crew that had the last man standing won.

We had a large, good natured black man in our team who took the lead. We lined up behind him and let him do the work. We didn't win, but it was the closest thing to fun that we did that week.

Thursday morning we paddled back to Coronado. By Thursday night our boat crew had shrunk, leaving five of us to carry the heavy boat, which bounced and sagged as we jogged due to the lack of support.

We received one man, "Joe," from another crew, bringing our boat crew back up to six. Joe was shorter than the rest of the crew which made it harder for him to reach the boat when we carried it overhead with arms extended.

Joe was a powerful man with an uncanny sense of humor, a strange cross between redneck and intellectual. He sang *Tom T. Hall* songs by heart, and on more than one occasion he had rescued the class, when the instructors demanded a song, by leading us in a chorus of "I like beer!"

Joe had been a Missouri State champion wrestler at 168 pounds. He could do fifteen single handed pull-ups, and early in first phase he won the BUD/S iron man competition.

Joe was positioned in front of me when we carried the boat. His presence added stability to the ever bouncing raft that seemed to be slowly losing air.

I didn't mean to step on his heels, and when he complained I told him that it was his fault for backing into me.

Our feet were soggy and blistered, and I'm certain the other tadpoles had sores like mine from running in wet boots. Joe had sores on his heels, and in his mind I was responsible. I can't say I was completely fearless when he turned and grabbed me by the collar, threatening, "I'm gonna' kick your ass!" but I was numb enough to pain and emotionless from lack of sleep, that I didn't give a shit.

"Yeah? Well you won't be able to do it just once. You'll have to do it again every time you see me, cuz' I won't give up until you're sick and tired of kicking my ass! How does that grab ya?"

Prompted by the other men Joe released me, and I apologized, adding, "I didn't mean to step on your heels."

Thursday night found us in the surf once again, but this time instead of being able to move, and replenish body warmth, we were instructed to lay, arm-in-arm, in the waves.

"If you can all stay in a straight line," the instructors told us, "you'll be allowed to return to your warm barracks and sleep."

The waves slammed us forward and swept us back dashing our hopes of maintaining any formation. Hours of freezing misery passed, and then the instructor in charge of the evolution changed the offer, "Okay, since you can't keep the line straight, I will secure this evolution and you can all go back to the barracks and sleep, if just one more man quits."

Over the next hour three tadpoles quit, but the instructors did not secure the evolution, in fact they told us to encourage the tadpole next to us to quit. The man to my left screamed repeatedly at the top of his lungs, in a faltering voice, "Quit Welch, quit!" His arm, locked together at the elbow with mine, shivered almost to the point of convulsions.

Rather than taking offense I found it entertaining. As cold as I was he was colder. Occasionally I yelled back just to stir the entertainment pot, it was like teasing an angry Chihuahua locked inside a car, and yet in no way was it personal.

Friday was more of the same, a timed long distance run in soft sand, the O-course, and a long cold swim in the ocean. Afterward the instructors assigned each of the boat crews to a wild goose chase. We were given a paper containing clues in the form of riddles. Each clue, if deciphered properly would lead us to a prize. There were five prizes in all, and once all five had been found we were to be secured from Hell Week. We jogged up and down the Silver Strand between Coronado and Imperial Beach with I.B.S. boats overhead, hunting down prizes. When we found the fifth prize, we were to wait for an instructor to come and secure us from Hell-Week.

We found the fifth prize around dawn on Saturday morning, and since there was no instructor around, we sat down in a circle with our backs to one another and fell asleep.

When the instructor found us he couldn't help laughing about how six men could fall asleep together in such a strange formation.

After Hell-Week, around twenty of the original class remained. Two setbacks from the previous class were added, bringing our number to twenty two.

The final weeks of first phase seemed easy, even mundane in comparison to Hell Week. We spent more time in class and study, although P.T. workouts were harder, swims were longer, and faster times were required in both the O-course and four mile timed runs. Our days were longer, and sleep—scant and illusive, but we had passed Hell Week and a great milestone lay behind us.

*

Several moments after I stopped talking I noticed Shellie staring straight ahead. I waved my hand in front of her face and called out, "Earth to Shellie, come-in!

Her eyes shifted slightly before she spoke, "Seems like an awful lot of punishment just for a trident insignia and a hundred and ten dollars a month, but you must have been in very good shape."

"We were in incredible shape."

"Looks like you still are."

"I still run six miles a day, five times a week. It's no longer just for exercise, it's therapeutic. When I finally have to quit I'm sure I'll go insane."

She laughed. "Speaking of insane, tell me more about this training."

Chapter Eight

Shitzen was his name! Not really, but swap a vowel here, and a consonant there, and you have something similar to the way I like to think of him.

Shitzen, one of the instructors, a large man by my standards, six foot, two, and over two-hundred pounds was a decorated Navy Seal, and Vietnam veteran. He led the class in P.T. in the mornings, and taught classes in stealth and concealment, counterinsurgency, and other subjects.

Shitzen began his classes with the phrase, "Gentlemen, the name of the game is 'R.P.P., Rape, Pillage and Plunder!'" for which he always received a hearty, "Hooyah!" The phrase never sat well with me, and I withheld my cheers for more worthy statements.

He often shared Viet Nam stories with the class. One of his stories had him walking down a berm between rice paddies with his automatic rifle slung over his shoulder.

"Three gooks were coming toward me," he related, "I knew they were gooks 'cuz they were making fun of me. So when they got close I pulled my M-16 off my shoulder, and shot the one in the middle square in the chest.

He dropped like a sack of potatoes!"

The class began to cheer, some of the men sprang to their feet, shouting, "Hooyah!"

When the cheering died, Shitzen continued, "The other two lit out as fast as they could go in opposite directions. I turned and ran after one of them. He tripped and fell off the berm. He was lying on his back in the rice paddy with his arms stretched in front of him begging for his life, sayin' 'please don't shoot me' in Vietnamese." With a sinister smile Shitzen demonstrated the man's outstretched arms. "So I fired a short burst in his chest. Blood squirted everywhere!"

Most of the class leaped to their feet, shouting and cheering.

Shitzen calmed the class and continued, "then I went looking for the last one. He seemed to have disappeared. I came to a cistern, a kind-of irrigation box used to flood the rice paddies. I could hear a hissing sound coming from the box, so I looked inside. The water was muddy, couldn't see a thing, but I noticed a reed sticking up, and I realized the gook was hiding under the water, breathing through the reed. I fired a burst into the water.

Blood gushed to the surface, and then his body floated up."

Again the class erupted with a cheer that slowly subsided until Shitzen's chuckle stood out above the clamor.

I raised my hand, and when Shitzen called on me I stood, and asked, "Do you mean to say that you shot three unarmed men for nothing more than making fun of you?"

Most of the class rose in an uproar, their opposition to my question louder than their cheering had been, with words like "idiot," and "asshole," and "shut the fuck up, Welch!"

Shitzen, with fist raised, started toward me. Several of the tadpoles held him back as he shouted over the noise, "They were gooks! You weren't there, you don't know what it was like! Guys like you didn't live very long. Your kind would get us all killed! We took guys like you out on patrol and they never made it back because we off'd them!"

Needless to say, class was dismissed early. Three of my fellow tadpoles told me privately that they agreed with me, but standing up to Shitzen was a stupid move.

I told them, "wrong thinking becomes the order of the day, if someone doesn't point out what's right."

Popularity wasn't my strong suit after that—in fact I was downright hated, even by those who had secretly agreed with me.

I pondered Shitzen's story long thereafter, wondering about his three victims. He may have been right, they could well have been Vietcong who masqueraded by day as civilians and attacked by night. Nonetheless his boasting reeked of bloodlust, and the game he dubbed "Rape Pillage and Plunder," appalled me.

*

Our off duty time, despite the long training hours for the remainder of first phase seemed monumental compared to hell-week.

One of the tadpoles, Proctor, rented stag films and a projector which he set up in the barrack's living room. Some of the guys participated. I can't say it was for lack of animal lust that I didn't join them, I had more than my share I just didn't need to feed my vices with that kind of nonsense.

I busied myself studying, writing letters, washing and ironing, and I stocked up on orange juice which I labeled "Welch" in felt pen, before storing it in the living room fridge. I drank it constantly in my spare time as recommended in our nutrition class, because our demanding daily grind depleted body nutrients, and orange juice supposedly helped replenish those nutrients.

I began to notice my bottles were vanishing, and like a hen counts her eggs, I counted quarts of orange juice. To remedy the situation, I stopped stocking orange juice except one bottle a day which I hoped to enjoy after the four mile timed run. The barracks was vacant during the runs, and the orange juice was safe I thought, but I was wrong.

I was usually the sixth, seventh or eighth man to cross the finish line in the four mile run, often within shouting distance of most of those ahead of me, and I always had enough time to return to the barracks, change cloths, and enjoy a bottle of orange juice before the last straggler crossed the finish line.

When my orange juice began to disappear I knew the thief was one of the two fastest runners, and I narrowed it to Proctor, since the other guy was good natured, not the stealing type.

I began to label the bottles, "Property of Welch, do not drink!" and I bettered my time on the runs, narrowing the gap between myself and Proctor to thirty seconds, hoping to catch him in the act.

53

I came close once, Proctor and another tadpole were in the barracks' living room after the run. As I entered I noticed my orange juice bottle lying empty in the waste basket. Proctor had a sinister look about him as he spoke to the other tadpole, "Wonder woman was my big sister's best friend.
I used to peek through the keyhole and watch her dress."

Proctor's words sounded like a ruse, yet almost convincing.

The other tadpole's eyes were on me as I pulled the empty bottle, still refrigerator-cold, from the waste basket. His expression told the story, *he was keeping silent for Proctor's sake.*

"Did you drink my orange juice, Proctor?" I asked.

"Would you mind not interrupting, we're talking!" Proctor's words made him sound assertive, perhaps angry.

I searched his coy, all knowing smile for traces of an orange juice mustache, and found none. "You should have been an actor, Proctor, you missed your calling." I turned and walked away, but before I reached the doorway, Proctor released a loud belch and followed with a chuckle.

His attitude and body language spoke louder than words, *"I've stolen your orange juice, and there's nothing you can do about it!"*

My mind was no longer on orange juice, I was baffled at the thought of Proctor watching Wonder Woman dress through the keyhole! To this day Proctor's words remain a mystery.

*

Shellie chuckled. "I think I know where this story is going. I can't believe that you would..."

"Don't say it!" I snapped, "I will never admit it!"

"You didn't!" she gasped.

"I told you, I'll never admit it!"

"Okay, so go on with your story."

*

Proctor hired a girl to take on some of the guys. She wasn't just gorgeous, she was the drop-dead, to die for type. I wasn't in on it, but the hallway clamor outside my room awakened me, and I got up to make a trip to the barracks' bathroom in my underwear. Some of the guys were lined up outside one room, but I, being barely awake, gave it little thought, as I made my way around the hall.

I was standing at the urinal when I felt her soft hair on my bare shoulder. In my astonishment I think I wet myself. "What are you doing in here?" I blurted in shock, half turning and pulling my shoulder from under her head. I was torn on whether to run and hide or stand my ground.

She glared back at me seemingly surprised, and I realized she was probably drunk.

A moment of awkward silence had hardly passed when the door swung open and in walked Joe dressed as if he had been out on the town. A whimsical smirk formed on his face as he glanced from her to me and back again. He pulled off his coat with the exuberance of a comedic stage actor, and lunged forward shouting, "I'll save ya' Sam!"

Waving the coat, he shooed her. "Back, back I say, back you vixen!"

She cringed and let out a mild squeal.

With a stroppy suddenness he turned back to me, flashing an expression that told me he was thoroughly entertained, and in the same fluid motion he slung the coat over my shoulders. "You're safe now Sam," he growled.

Perhaps it was my expression, or the absence thereof that set him ablaze with laughter. Stepping back, he swatted the girl on the ass and forced words laced with mirth, "Okay, this is not a co-ed bathroom get the hell out of here!"

She offered no reply, and as she left, Joe followed her for a couple of steps before returning and yanking the coat from my shoulders. "I'll take my coat, thank you!"

The next moment found me standing tense in front of a urinal alone in an invisible cloud of fading perfume, unable to pee, asking myself if what just happened really happened, or if I had wet myself for nothing?

The following day Shitzen scolded the class, "I heard through the grape vine that you had a girl in the barracks, and you guys didn't even bother to call me! So who all was in on it, or maybe I should ask who wasn't in on it?"

Proctor spoke up, "Welch and Joe weren't in on it!"

"Welch is an idiot, but why weren't you in on it, Joe?" Shitzen asked.

"Well, it's like this," Joe's voice had that un-refutable, all-knowing quality, "I like to have my fun, but I don't like to mix mine around with everyone else's!" A few chuckles followed, but overall the response was mild, although in my mind Joe's statement was huge.

*

"Ugh!" Shellie grimaced. "I can't even imagine that. She must have been really sore the next day."

"Huh? Oh! I wouldn't know." A myriad of thoughts cluttered my mind, vaginal callouses and the like, but I quickly dismissed them, and took a sip of Coke as if to wash a bad taste from my mouth and move on. "Okay, so tell me about you."

"No! I'm enjoying your story, please go on."

*

Proctor's popularity was immense, and my sense of timing more than a little off, but I had one bottle of orange juice left. This time I decided to add a little something to the label, so instead of marking it, "Welch's, do not drink!" I wrote, "Property of Sam Welch, Please do not drink!"

Did I really think that Proctor wouldn't drink it? I wasn't one hundred percent sure that Proctor was the culprit, but I was determined to find out!

Instead of returning to the barracks after the four mile run, I went straight to class. Proctor was a no-show, and after role call the instructor asked if anybody knew where he was?

One of the tadpoles raised his hand and said, "Proctor's sick, he's still in the barracks vomiting. He says 'somebody peed in his orange juice!'"

The class seemed to groan in unison, following with comments like, "who would pee in someone's orange juice?" and "That's a pretty low thing to do!"

"No way!" I muttered, realizing that Proctor was not only a thief but a politician as well.

A few minutes later Proctor entered the room and sat down. I surveyed his enraged glare, and returned a casual smile. He looked more than just a little pale, and I didn't need a crystal ball to know that his rumor about me peeing in his orange juice was about to add more credibility to my reputation as the most hated man in BUD/S training.

Shortly thereafter, I was summoned to speak with the main instructor for our phase.

"You're probably wondering why we're having this meeting," he said.

"Why, is something wrong?" I asked.

"Well, according to Proctor, you peed in his orange juice."

"I did no such thing!" I flatly stated, "in fact, I'm certain Proctor has never bought orange juice, but he constantly steals mine and drinks it! Why don't you ask Proctor to produce some receipts for his orange juice?" I realized I was beginning to sound agitated, I softened my tone, "Nope!

Proctor's not only a thief, he's a liar!"

"I think I'm beginning to get the picture here. You can go Welch."

It wasn't long before Proctor confronted me privately, "You peed in the orange juice, you sick son of a bitch!" His fists were clenched, and he stood within striking distance.

I straightened and held my position. "Allegedly!"

"What?"

"Allegedly," I repeated, "It's never been established that I peed in any orange juice!" I couldn't help feeling mildly amused at his lack of composure.

"Oh you did it all right!" he snapped, "you peed in the orange juice, you filthy son of a bitch."

"So now it's 'the' orange juice."

"What the hell do you mean?" he demanded.

"First it was my orange juice, then you told everyone that I peed in 'your' orange juice, but now it's 'the' orange juice! You need to get your facts straight, Proctor!"

"It was more than just orange juice!" The venom in his voice seemed to be increasing.

I couldn't resist a little humor. "Okay, so we're talking about a cocktail here."

"I don't know what the fuck you're trying to say, but I know it takes a warped individual to pee in a bottle of orange juice." He stepped closer as if to provoke a fight, a fight from which I would not have backed down.

"Well, Proctor this wouldn't be an issue if you weren't a thief, would it?" I stood there a moment allowing him the opportunity to take a swing, and when it didn't happen I walked away.

He shouted after me, "the next time you leave orange juice in the fridge I'm going to pee in it!"

"Don't worry, I've learned my lesson," I shouted back.

Chapter Nine

W hen first phase ended the rumors became official, we were to be the first pilot class. We would combine with the class ahead of us for the diving phase of training.

Land Warfare, which was normally second phase would become our third phase.

*

The diving phase began with a series of familiarization classes, and practical training evolutions using open circuit SCUBA gear. In one of the evolutions we were instructed to sit at the bottom of the pool using our SCUBA tanks and regulator, while the instructors descended on us, turning off our tanks, disconnecting our hoses, and pulling off our masks. The important thing was to remain calm while re-donning masks, reconnecting hoses and turning on tanks.

I was a natural, an immediate diving addict. I had never considered diving, but once I started I knew I would never stop.

The instructors, who remembered me from Practical Lifesaving, were shocked at my ability to relax while reassembling my dive gear underwater. I could even breathe from a disconnected tank when I had to by cupping my hand and collecting bubbles.

We began the diving phase with open circuit SCUBA, and later progressed to semi closed, and closed circuit systems. The difference between open and closed circuit SCUBA is that closed circuit SCUBA emits no bubbles making the diver undetectable underwater. With Open Circuit SCUBA the diver breathes atmospheric air, but with closed systems the diver breathes oxygen.

Oxygen becomes toxic at one atmosphere of pressure which makes it dangerous for the diver to descend below thirty three feet.

Sam Welch

The Emerson Closed Circuit System, developed in 1948, was somewhat antiquated, and we were told that the Navy was about to transition to a newer and better system.

The Emerson was light, and built inside a solid canvas jacket with a zipper, locking straps and two counter lungs in the front. The back part of the rig had a built-in fiberglass backpack which held a small oxygen bottle and scrubber canister filled with a granulated chemical to filter the CO_2 from the spent oxygen. Instead of a regulator, the Emerson had a mouthpiece with a shutoff valve that could be flipped like a light switch to prevent water from entering the mouthpiece and contaminating the scrubber. If water entered the scrubber and mixed with the granulated chemical, the breathing mixture could be fatal to the diver.

After diving with the Emerson most of the tadpoles complained of feeling sluggish, even sick. I was just the opposite, and during a four mile timed run after diving with the Emerson, I came in second, beating my best time by more than two minutes.

The runs, long swims and O-course continued and grew more demanding during second phase but I awakened each morning optimistic. I remained optimistic until one day in January of 1977.

The instructors joked about the fifty foot waves that morning, the kind of waves that erode the California shoreline, ruining beach homes, shattering multi-million dollar dreams. In their minds our training was far too lax, and it was time to separate the men from the boys.

The plan was to drop us off in pairs three miles off the coast of Coronado for an underwater compass swim to the beach using the Emerson.

The majority of the tadpoles in both classes refused to go.

The word from the instructors was that all who refused would be court-marshalled for disobeying a direct order. I was one of the eight who agreed to go.

They paired me up with Gonzales since my regular dive partner, and Gonzales' partner had refused the dive.

The instructors had to arrange a 120 foot landing ship, because the eighty footer normally used for ocean dives could not make it over the bar.

The ship was designed for transporting tanks and heavy equipment. It had a control cabin to the rear that overlooked an open cargo hold with high walls and a drop gate in the front.

When we reached the open ocean we were tossed about mercilessly as waves crashed over the back and sides of the ship.

The Coxswain waited for a low series before dropping the gate, and then slowly backed the ship into the oncoming swells. We held onto the chains on the side of the gate as waves crashed over the cabin, partially filling the cargo hold. Between waves we did buddy checks and waited for the right moment to jump.

"I'm sorry for the way I've treated you." Gonzales' voice was raised competing with the vibration of the engine and the crashing ocean as he quivered beside me, both of us clinging to the chain on the drop gate.

In my seasick state, I hadn't given it any thought, and when I did think about it, he hadn't treated me any worse than the other tadpoles. "No problem," I replied, trying to produce a smile and hold back breakfast at the same time.

"Friends?" He found a free hand and offered it.

"I could really use one!" I met his hand with the most awkward of grips while we clung to the chain.

"I have to know something," he said.

"Sure, what?"

"Would you save me if I got in trouble?"

"Of course I would," I assured him, "but just stay down, grab sand, and whatever you do don't surface in the surf zone, and we'll be fine." As calming as I tried to sound I wasn't at all sure of myself.

"Are you scared? 'Cuz I'm really scared!"

"I'm scared shitless," I admitted, "but we'll be fine."

"You don't understand I think I'm going to die today!" His face was ashen, his breaths short, his eyes reflected a certain desperation that no amount of reassurance could change.

"Bullshit!" I half shouted, competing with the surf, as well as his death notion. "We'll be fine. Don't let yourself think that way!"

After a last minute double check on our gear, which included the eight foot of buddy line that latched us together, as well as a ridiculous twenty five feet of line with a buoy on the end that extended from the buddy line, we were ready to go.

When the Coxswain signaled a low series we jumped arm in arm from the lift gate into the water. Diving immediately we swam to clear the gate and prevent it from slamming down on us.

The water turbidity was so dense that although we remained arm in arm, my left arm locked at the elbow with his right, we were unable to see each other. I had to hold the compass board/depth gauge mere inches from my face in order to see it and maintain depth and direction.

With the passing swells our depth fluctuated from ten feet to sixty feet, leaving me more than a little uneasy about breathing pure oxygen which becomes toxic at thirty three feet.

When we reached the surf zone, where the waves began to break above us, I knew that we were still a mile off shore. The surf zone was a game changer, we were swept forward grazing the sandy bottom with frightening speed as each incoming wave burst with a deafening sound casting dark shadows over the impermeable wash. Suddenly, and no less furious the returning surge repeatedly struck us, engulfing us in a lighter shade of darkness, carrying with it sand and pebbles that stung my lips and cheeks, while slamming us back, compelling us to tuck our heads in a futile attempt to protect ourselves and maintain what little ground we had gained. The cycle continued relentlessly, and with each onslaught I prayed that we wouldn't be smashed headfirst into a rock or drifting log.

We had been fighting the surf for some time when I found myself unable to kick, the surge began sweeping me around like a rag doll. I realized my legs had become tangled in the buoy line. I needed to free my hands in order to untangle my legs. I had no way to explain my situation to Gonzales. As I slipped my arm from our arm lock I could only hope that he would stay down until I could free my legs and rejoin him.

I had barely untangled my legs when Gonzales began tugging on the buddy line. Three solid tugs was the distress signal—he was in trouble! I had to surface and help him.

Standard Operating Procedure dictated that the first course of action in such situations was to inflate your dive partner's buoyancy compensator which was nothing more than an inflatable horse-collar life-vest. It was a bad plan for this kind of surf.

Inflating the vest was as simple as pulling a string, or lanyard on the diver's chest which popped a CO_2 cartridge causing the vest to fill.

I swam to the surface where the daylight immediately blinded me. Gonzales was still tugging on the line. As my eyes began to adjust I could make out his head and face, his eyes fastened on me. His mask was gone, his expression—one of hopelessness. I skulled toward him, reaching, feeling for the lanyard, but not finding it, and then my eyes acclimating, took in the bigger picture. We were being swept rapidly into the crest of a massive oncoming wave that towered perhaps fifty feet above us. I was stunned for a moment, beyond fear, unable to believe my eyes when the wave struck with the fury of a locomotive. I was tossed and thrashed like a handkerchief in a clothes dryer. My wind was knocked from me, I had no idea which way was up, and my mouthpiece was gone from my mouth. Gonzales was already tugging on the line, and I was still in a daze. I collected my senses and felt for my mouthpiece. I knew water had seeped in and contaminated the scrubber, the oxygen was probably lethal, and could no longer be breathed. When I found the mouthpiece I immediately shut off the valve, thinking I would only breathe it as a last resort. My mask was gone, and I had no idea what else I had lost. Gonzales continued to tug, which led me to think he was in a better state of mind than I was.

I surfaced again, catching my breath as I swam toward him. He looked more distraught than before. As I felt for the lanyard I realized we were being swept rapidly into another wave, equal to, or larger than the previous one. I was still feeling for the lanyard when the wave struck with unbelievable fury.

At first I thought I was dead, but when I stopped tumbling I realized I was alive, and desperately in need of air.

Not knowing which way was up, I followed the bubbles. A layer of foam, about eight inches deep, covered the water. I was unable to rise above the foam in order to get a breath. I felt for my life vest, but it was missing, the buddy line was gone and so was Gonzales. Another wave hit, and another, and still I could not get to the surface. I was about to try my luck with the contaminated Emerson when it dawned on me that I had lost my fins, and my weight belt was holding me down.

I dropped the weight belt and scrambled above the foam for the sweetest breath I had ever drawn, and then as quickly, I dove and clutched the sandy bottom.

When the next wave passed I surfaced for air, and once I had filled my lungs, I dove, clenching sand with my fists until the following wave had passed. I repeated the process again and again, realizing my limitations, surfacing just behind the crest of the wave, feeling the spray from each massive crash that spattered me with large droplets followed by lighter mist, each time remaining afloat until the next oncoming breaker forced me to dive.

With every following wake the shoreline grew closer until I felt the sand beneath my feet.

From shore I looked around for Gonzales, hoping against hope that he had made it safely. A glance at my gear told me that my fins, mask, life vest and K-bar knife were gone. I had only the Emerson rig, and the tan Navy issue shorts which I was wearing.

I noticed two instructors about a hundred yards away, and I hurried to tell them that I had lost Gonzales. They alerted the rest of the Navy of the situation by means of a hand radio. Within minutes Instructors and tadpoles alike scoured the shoreline searching for Gonzales. I too remained on the beach searching.

I can't say whether I was sorrier for Gonzales when I learned of his passing, or for myself for having found a friend, and lost him as quickly. I would have given all my meager worldly belongings if rather than seeing his lifeless body rolling in the surf, tangled in the buoy line, I could have shaken his hand and said, *thank God you made it my friend!*

The instructors gave him C.P.R., but it was to no avail.

Our Commanding Officer, along with some of the other officers met me near the barracks on my way up from the beach. One of Gonzales' friends was with them. The C.O. informed me that C.P.R. and life support had failed. "Gonzales didn't make it. So how did you get those cuts on your face, Welch?" he asked.

I was more than a little surprised at the suspicion in his eyes. "Cuts on my face?"

"Your nose is split wide open, you're bleeding!"

I touched my nose and looked at my hand. He was right, I was bleeding. "I have no idea." I replied.

"How can you not know how your face got cut up?"

The ridicule in his words angered me. "You put us out there in that kind of surf, and then you ask, 'how can I not know how my face got cut up?'"

"What do you mean by 'that kind of surf? It's my understanding that everyone else made it in safely!"

I realized that the left hand didn't know what the right hand was doing.

"Have you seen the ocean today, Sir?"

"Damn it Welch," he shouted, "I've got a dead man on my hands, and I want to know who's to blame!"

65

"Whose idea was it to put us out there today, and whose idea was it to have us drag buoys around, to warn boats that divers are below, on a day when boats can't even get out on the ocean?" I said in a voice intended to let him know that I was the only one who had a right to be angry.

"Lieutenant Johns is the Officer of the Day, I suppose it was his idea."

I noticed Lieutenant Johns standing a few feet behind the C.O. I pointed directly at Johns and blurted, "It's his fault, look no further!"

Ignoring my words, the C.O. continued, "It's my understanding that you and Gonzales were enemies?"

"That's not true!"

Gonzales' friend stepped forward, "Oh yes it is!"

"Welch," the C.O. began sternly, "you will consider yourself under house arrest, under suspicion of murder, and confine yourself to the barracks, however, you will be required to make all the classes, dives and evolutions with your class until all of the evidence has been gathered and investigated. Until further notice, you will go nowhere without authorization, do you understand?

"Murder?"

"You heard me, Welch! Do you understand?

"Yes sir, I think I understand."

"Good, leave the Emerson Rig here, change your clothes and hurry to the BUD/S Command Building for a debriefing."

I was shown to a conference room in the BUD/S Command Building where I was given pen and tablet, and told to write everything I could remember from that morning until the end of the fateful evolution. After writing my statement, I repeated my story over and over in a conference room full of J.A.G. (Judge Advocate General) attorneys, N.I.S. (Naval Investigative Service) personnel, and the Commanding and Executive Officers. I answered all of their questions honestly, giving the same answers to the same questions that popped up repeatedly.

That afternoon I was excused from the interrogations to make a dive with the class. The dive was made in the bay because the ocean was deemed too dangerous.

My regular dive partner had refused to dive with me, and so I was assigned Gonzales' former dive partner from that time on. The consensus throughout the class seemed to support my guilt, and a lot of the guys refused to speak to me.

Ironically, I received support from the most unlikely person. Proctor slapped me gently on the back, and said, "I want you to know I'm sorry that happened to you."

"Everyone else seems to think it's my fault," I said.

"They all know how rough the ocean was, that's why everyone refused to go. What happened to you could have happened to anybody."

Proctor's words brought tears to my eyes, the hard to control kind of tears that come with those embarrassing sobs and involuntary hiccup-like jerks.

After the dive I was called back to the conference room for more debriefing.

The following day I was excused from class for an appointment with the J.A.G. attorney who was assigned to my case. He was a Lieutenant Commander, friendly and personable.

"I've read your story," he began, "and I can't believe they dropped you guys off in the ocean in that kind of surf. Just for your information, when all the findings are on the table, I'm certain you'll be cleared of any wrongdoing, but you'll never be allowed to graduate from BUD/S."

"But, I've been doing very well," I protested. "How could they stop me from graduating if I don't slip up?" I noticed his expression, his head shaking as I spoke, and I realized that he knew more about the inner politics of BUD/S than I had ever imagined.

"Mark my words, even if you give it your best, and these charges are dropped, they will find some way to get you out! You are an embarrassment to them, and you can rest assured they will railroad you out of the training."

It was a lot for me to swallow. I couldn't help hoping that he was wrong. All of the months of effort, cold and suffering, was it all for nothing? What of my wife, and soon-coming child? Would I be able to make enough money to support them, let alone ever see my wife again? How would I continue to pay for my property without hazardous duty pay? What about the worst case scenario? Murder! What if I were convicted of murder?

I noticed a disparaging tremble in my own voice. "Until that day, I'll give it everything I have. I won't make it easy for them!"

The J.A.G. attorney's expression went from sad to optimistic. "I do have some good news, although they haven't made it public yet, and they may never make it public, here are pictures of your diving rig. Notice that the whole side of the canvas jacket where the buddy line attached holding you and Gonzales together, has been ripped away. That's how you lost him, or he lost you."

He handed me another picture, it was Gonzales' Emerson Rig. "Notice the buddy line is still attached to the piece of canvas that was ripped from your Emerson Rig. It took tremendous force to rip that canvas! So far all of the evidence supports your story, and Gonzales suffered no fatal contusions, he simply drowned, but don't expect them to clear you any time soon—they need a scapegoat. That being said, these charges should never have been pressed, and I'm fairly confident this case will never go to trial." Three days after the accident I was summoned by the Commanding Officer. I knocked on his office door frame, and when beckoned I entered and saluted.

"At ease Welch, have a seat." He cast me that friendly, fake half-smile intended to make an adversary feel comfortable in an uncomfortable situation, and motioned to the chair in front of his desk.

I lowered myself into the chair, and thought how inappropriate and insincere the words, "at ease" seemed, coming from him, at a time like this.

"I called you here to let you know you are no longer under house arrest. The test results have come back on the Emerson Rigs. Your Emerson Rig had very little water inside. The mouthpiece valve was closed which prevented water from flooding the scrubber just as you said in your statement. This tells me that you maintained calm in a tragic situation. Gonzales' Rig, on the other hand was flooded. He panicked, and that's why he drowned. I've also learned that he panicked on a previous dive and had to be rescued. As you probably know, the side of your rig was torn—most likely by the wave that separated the two of you, which supports your statement as well."

I found myself listening to his words with no less callous than the tone with which he pronounced them. An apology might have been nice, but that too would have seemed meaningless. In short, I was numb to the bullshit!

"Gonzales had two families," he continued.

"How so?" I asked, as I pondered whether taking me off house arrest would do anything to curtail the cloud of suspicion that followed me.

"He had a birth mother, who gave him and his brother up for adoption. She had children after the adoption, who are his blood siblings. He also has an adopted family. The two families will be here tomorrow afternoon, his birth family will be here at one P.M., and his adopted parents will be here at three. I need you to explain to them what happened. I'll have you pulled out of class when they get here. That is all Welch!"

The following afternoon I sat with the two families, telling and reliving my story, crying with them as they cried, and feeling as helpless to offer them comfort as I had been to rescue Gonzales.

Chapter Ten

That's horrible!" Shellie's outburst rose over the restaurant chatter. Realizing that she had called attention to herself, she tucked her head and began to whisper, "I mean It was bad enough that Gonzales died, but it's horrible that you had to go through all of that." "Things didn't get much better after that." I said.

"You don't have to tell me if you don't want to," she offered, although her eyes begged for me to continue.

I resumed my story, knowing it was good to let it out once in a while.

*

Second Phase ended and third phase, "Land Warfare" began. We were lucky to get three hours of sleep at night. We drilled on counterinsurgency, and infiltrating villages, stream and river crossing, sneak attacks, night attacks, hasty ambushes, and we learned to fire, breakdown and reassemble all kinds of weapons.

Faster times were demanded in the O-Course, timed runs, and timed swims.

I improved my swim times dramatically, forcing myself beyond what I thought was possible. I also improved my time on the runs, although running had never been my weak point.

Ironically it was on the timed runs that I began to notice the J.A.G. attorney's words played out, in the instructor's efforts to force me from the training. During several of the timed runs, the instructors announced the cutoff just before I crossed the finish line, when I knew beyond a doubt that I had beat the cutoff time.

The instructors, as well as myself, were aware of the effort to railroad me, and once in a while I received a slap on the back and a whisper of support.

One incident that left me in shock occurred when our First Phase instructor interrupted one of Shitzen's classes and asked if he could say something. When Shitzen gave him the floor he stepped in front of the class and said, "I've heard over and over what an idiot Welch is. Welch isn't an idiot! Those of you who think he is should read the three page statement he wrote after Gonzales' death. That's all I wanted to say." He thanked Shitzen and left as abruptly as he entered.

Shitzen glanced around the class, a sarcastic smile on his lips, "I have my own thoughts on the matter!"

His words inspired a round of laughter which had little effect on me. I was not surprised by the overwhelming majority who stood against me, I was surprised by that rare individual who stood on my behalf.

*

Several weeks into third phase I was summoned by the Commanding Officer.

"We've been reviewing your file Welch," he began with a callous air that made me wonder if this was the beginning of the end, and then he continued with, "and it's come to my attention that you failed a practical lifesaving exam in first phase, therefore I've scheduled a practical lifesaving exam for this afternoon. Be at the Base Pool at 1600 hours. Petty Officer
Shitzen will be administering that exam."

I don't know why I didn't let on to the C.O. that I could see holes in his motives big enough to drive a truck through, I simply complied, and at 1600 hours I found Shitzen, along with the Senior Chief and Petty Officer Flanerty waiting for me at the pool.

The Senior Chief wasted no time in explaining the evolution, "Okay, Welch, you recall the 'arm drag, chin tilt and cross chest carry' from first phase, right?"

"Yes, I do," I replied. The memory produced a bitter taste in my mouth.

Sam Welch

"Petty Officer Shitzen will represent a drowning person, and you will swim out and rescue him using the arm drag, chin tilt and cross chest carry, do you understand?"

"Let's get this over with!" Shitzen called out in an anxious voice, with a smile that I knew only too well as his rape, pillage, and plunder expression. After pulling his shirt off, and tossing it aside, he dove into the pool and waited while I removed my shirt and boots. Before I got my second boot off he called out angrily, "come-on Welch, we're waiting!"

When I was ready I positioned myself on the edge of the pool. I glanced at the Senior Chief, awaiting his nod, just to show Shitzen that he wasn't calling the shots.

As the Senior Chief gave the nod, I noticed the anticipation in he and Flanerty's expressions, as if they were watching the climax of a blockbuster film just before the bad guy gets it, and it served to confirm my suspicions that this was more than a practical lifesaving exam.

Shitzen was twenty feet out. I dove and glided toward him. Grabbing his wrist, I pulled him upward. I was shifting from chin tilt to cross chest carry when he turned on me, locking his elbow around my neck, and his legs in a scissor hold around my chest.

I tucked my chin to keep him from strangling me, just as he renewed his grip with his forearm at throat level and latched it with his opposite arm in an obvious attempt to choke me.

I skulled downward with my hands, and we sank rapidly.

We were about ten feet deep when Shitzen released his choke hold on my neck. He used his hands to skull upward while maintaining his scissor hold around my chest with his legs. His efforts to reach the surface while pulling me upward failed, and we continued to sink until I found myself sitting, fully relaxed on the bottom, twenty feet deep.

Releasing his scissor hold he pushed off my shoulder with his foot and headed for the surface.

A harsh realization came over me, *if Shitzen catches his breath, I might as well kiss my ass goodbye!* Pushing off the bottom, I followed him reluctantly upward, wondering if I could really do what I knew I had to do.

His face was about to break the surface when I grabbed his ankle and jerked him back down. I'll never forget the "glubglubglub" sound or the sight of bubbles escaping from his mouth as I grabbed the back of his trunks and pulled myself up while pulling him down. I threw my forearm around his throat and held him while he thrashed wildly in an obvious state of panic.

I don't know how often the prey rises victorious over the predator, seldom I suppose. I was that one exception, and I was well aware that if I let up for an instant, Shitzen would mercilessly turn the tables on me.

What should have felt good lacked the triumphal luster that one would expect or deserve, but it was not a game, it was a matter of self-preservation nothing more, nothing less.

When Shitzen's arms went limp I thought he was faking, and I could only wonder how this tough Navy Seal, this master of rape, pillage and plunder could turn out to be such a pussy!

A second glance told me he was passive, so I went with the chin tilt and the cross chest carry.

The Senior Chief and Flanerty were on their knees leaning over the edge of the pool, clamoring frantically, with outstretched arms when I swam in with Shitzen.

I pushed while they pulled, and together we were able to get Shitzen's unconscious form from the water to the pool deck.

Flanerty administered one chest compression and lowered his head to begin mouth to mouth when Shitzen spat up a small geyser of water and immediately began swinging, striking Flanerty at least once.

The Senior Chief and Flanerty stepped back as Shitzen rose to his feet cursing and choking.

"You'd better go in the locker room and get yourself straightened out, Shitzen," the Senior Chief said, pointing.

Shitzen walked away choking, leaving a trail of water, foul language, and wet footprints.

The Senior Chief glanced at me, and then at Flanerty, "Okay Flanerty, let's see if he can rescue you!"

"Not me Senior Chief, I'm not going out there with him!"

"Flanerty!" The Senior Chief half shouted, "that's a direct order, get your ass out there now!"

Flanerty nodded, threw off his shirt, and dove in.

When he was ready I swam out after him, performing the arm drag, chin tilt and cross chest carry.

About ten feet from the edge of the pool I felt Flanerty start to turn on me. I wasn't about to allow any more Shitzen tactics! I tightened my arm on his chest and threw my free arm around his neck, pulling him under. He stopped fighting almost immediately, and showed me his arms in a gesture of surrender. I released him, and with a chin tilt and cross chest carry I brought him to the surface, and on to the edge of the pool.

"He did good Senior Chief," Flanerty called out.

"Let's see him do it again." The Senior Chief's voice carried more than a hint of anger.

"I don't know what this is all about!" Flanerty complained in a whisper, shaking his head as he pushed off the side of the pool.

I swam out after Flanerty, repeating the rescue sequence. When he started to turn on me I tightened my hold on his chest, and continued swimming.

I could tell that Flanerty meant me no harm, as he relaxed and allowed me to continue.

When we reached the side of the pool, Flanerty called out once again, "He did good Senior Chief!"

I began to wonder if the Senior Chief would be my next rescue, and I was savoring that thought when Shitzen's voice cut in, "stay out there, you're not done yet, you little son of a bitch!"

I turned and watched Shitzen striding, almost stomping from the locker room to the pool, his every action laced with violent emotion, mingled with an occasional cough. He carried a wadded towel in his left hand, which he threw down hard onto the deck before diving into the water.

Surfacing, he called to me, "Get out here you little son of a bitch!"

I couldn't help but wonder what made him think he would fare any better this time than he had the time before.

As I approached he took a swing at me, which I blocked. I dove, attempting to get ahold of him from underwater, but he kicked at me repeatedly in a frantic effort to escape. I released him and re-surfaced, keeping a safe distance. Once again he swung and missed. In return I flipped water in his face.

"All right," the Senior Chief shouted, "both of you get out of the pool!"

After pulling myself from the pool I ignored Shitzen's angry gaze, he was little more than a small player in a game that I had already given up on. The ball was in their court, and the question they had to answer was, did I fail the practical lifesaving exam or not? The answer meant little to me, I had moved beyond it into the roll-with-the-punches mode, and I gave little thought to what lay ahead. Unfortunately, my altercation with Shitzen gave ammunition to my adversaries who thought that I had drowned Gonzales. The following day I received a summons from the Commanding Officer. I knew my days at BUD/S were drawing to a close, and I had already abandoned hope of graduating. The questions that haunted me were, how much longer would they drag this out, how much more bullshit was I expected to endure before I was given the final axe, and what sort of justification for cutting me from training would the C.O. pull from his bag of ridiculous tricks?

After motioning for me to be seated, the C.O. announced, "I've received mixed reports on whether you passed the Practical Lifesaving exam, therefore we'll have to hold a hearing to decide your future here at

BUD/S. That hearing will convene one week from today. You will not go to

San Clemente Island with your class. You will remain here at BUD/S and be assigned temporary additional duties to whatever department your rating qualifies you to work in."

Chapter Eleven

Shellie shook her head. "You can't say they weren't creative in their efforts to get rid of you. I think I would have just got it over with and rang the bell."

I shook my head as well. "I couldn't ring the bell, too much of my heart and soul had been poured into the training, not just for my own sake, but for the sake of my wife and our soon-coming child." "Okay, so what happened?"

*

I was assigned temporary additional duty in the Admin Office where my duties varied. I ran errands and delivered records between Admin and the legal office, where I became acquainted with the legal yeoman, although not by name.

I noticed my service record always lying open on a table in the legal office and one day I asked why that particular record was always open on the table.

The yeoman responded with, "that's the guy that murdered his dive partner, you must have heard about it."

My words came more as a plea from my heart than an objection, "That's my service record, and no one ever tried harder to save anyone than I tried to save Gonzales. It's not fair to me that I should be treated like this, or thought of as a murderer."

"I'm sorry," he said, "I don't know what to say."

"I just needed to say that I am a real person with real feelings, who would have died to save Gonzales, and even now I would give anything to bring him back, but I can't! The worst part is that no one knows, cares, understands or even wants to believe me!"

Unfortunately, the Yeoman's sentiments seemed to follow me over my remaining years in the Navy. No matter where I went, someone always popped up who knew me as the guy who murdered my dive partner.

The week came and went rapidly, serving only one good purpose, it afforded me the opportunity to take the exam for third class petty officer, although I didn't really have time to study.

When the hearing convened to determine whether I had passed the practical lifesaving exam, I was told to wait outside the doors of the conference room where the hearing was held. Present inside were the Commanding Officers and Executive Officers of both the BUD/S Command, and the Naval Amphibious Base at Coronado. The BUD/S instructors were also present.

I waited patiently for perhaps an hour before they called me in.

The Commanding Officer for BUD/S addressed me. "Welch, I've got good news and bad news! Which would you like to hear first?" "I'm not sure I care at this point," I said.

"Well, the good news is, you passed the Practical Lifesaving Exam. The bad news is, that since you've missed a week of training, you won't be allowed to graduate with your class."

"Then you're going to set me back to the beginning of third phase in the next class?"

"No, you'll have to begin the training over again."

"That's odd," I said, not really surprised, just digging for clarification, "because up to this point, your rule for setbacks has always been to pick them up after the end of the last completed phase."

"In your case, Welch, we're setting a precedence because you've come too far, but we'll keep a billet open for you in the next available class."

I chuckled, "You'd never allow me to complete the training even if I started from the beginning."

"That's not true Welch, we will hold no prejudice against you, but if you decide not to accept our offer, then ring the bell on your way out!"

"Your offer to begin over again is not a viable offer, and the bell is for quitters. I have never quit, and I refuse to ring that bell!"

"Then this hearing is over!" the C.O. said, smacking a little wooden hammer onto a gavel.

Shitzen caught up with me in the hallway and began shouting in my ear like a drill sergeant, "Ring the bell, ring that fucking bell right now Welch!"

"Leave him alone Shitzen," the C.O. demanded sharply, "he doesn't have to ring the bell if he doesn't want to."

Shitzen walked away muttering angrily.

The C.O. leaned close to my ear, and whispered, "You know Welch, if the truth were known, today we'd probably be giving you a medal instead of dis-enrolling you, but unfortunately for you the truth will never be known!"

Chapter Twelve

hellie shook her head. "That's a sad story. You didn't go out and get drunk afterward, did you?"

S"Funny you should say that, although I prefer the phrase 'pleasantly buzzed.'"

She chuckled. "You probably got yourself in trouble as well!" "Fake cowboys!" I recalled audibly.

"Fake cowboys?"

"You know, the ones that don't know nothin' about horses or cows, they just dress up in Wranglers, hats and boots to go out line-dancing, wowing all the fake cowgirls while drawling phrases like 'ya'all, and ma'am, and such.'"

"Wowing all the fake cowgirls?" She gasped, adding with a smile, "Watch it buster, you're treading on some pretty shaky ground, and there's nothing wrong with line-dancing!"

*

Wednesday night was Country Western Night at the base's Enlisted Club, and a lot of marines from the surrounding bases dressed up as cowboys and came out to enjoy the festivity. They didn't like sailors, and they didn't like anyone who wasn't wearing boots and a hat, and when they couldn't find either they fought amongst themselves.

I was drowning my sorrows with a few friends who had been disenrolled from BUD/S for medical reasons.

A group of cowboys, seven in all, followed me into the restroom. One of them, a stocky, sawed off fellow, bumped me and continued to press his chest against me, while I stood at the urinal intending to relieve myself.

With the bill of his hat pressed against my neck he growled, "You look like a fucking hippie!"

His friends who were scattered about, leaning against the walls and stall doors, began to laugh.

I realized he was referring to my three day beard which I had grown to show the Navy that I was sick of the bullshit. "Do you mind, I'm trying to pee!" I told him. My words sparked a new round of laughter from his friends.

Pressing his chest harder against me, he bellowed louder, "Maybe you didn't hear me sod-buster, I said, 'you look like a fucking hippie!'"

His friends chuckled again. One of them called out, "You tell him Wilbur!"

Zipping myself up, and wondering if it was cowboy initiation night, I warned, "I'm not going to tell you again, Orville to leave me alone."

His eyes enlarged with rage. "The name's Wilbur, and you don't listen very well..."

I caught him by the throat with the nap of my hand, silencing him in mid-sentence. It was indeed cowboy initiation night!

Half-carrying him by the neck, into the stall behind us, I slammed his head against the rim of the toilet and baptized him in the sobering reality that some previous cowboy had thoughtfully left behind.

Wilbur never emerged from the stall while I was there, but I know he survived because I could hear him vomiting. In all the excitement I forgot I had to pee.

Three of my friends, who had watched the cowboys follow me in, entered the restroom. They dragged me off of Wilbur, and out of the stall, explaining to the group of cowboys, "We're really sorry, he's had too much to drink."

I was much less humble than my friends as I sang those cowboys a chorus of "Mamma don't let your cowboys grow up to be babies!" Twice I broke free, although my friends recaptured me, moving me closer to the door. I was ready to take on the whole bunch. "I've ridden more horses, castrated and branded more steers, milked more cows, and built more fence than all of you fake cowboys combined!" I boasted.

Sam Welch

My comment about milking cows struck them as funny. "That's woman's work!" exclaimed one. Another cracked a sheep joke at my expense, too rude to repeat, to which I answered, "you oughta' know, right,

Ewe?"

A couple of them took swipes at me, and ripped my shirt off before my friends could get me out the door. When my friends released me I was about to go back in, but after they explained how foolish that would be, and how fortunate I was that those cowboys didn't gang up on me, I thought better of it, and returned to the barracks.

*

Shellie took another sip of her coke, the cowboy story didn't seem to interest her. "So where did you go after BUD/S?"

"They transferred me to HC-1, Detachment 2, which was a helicopter squadron that deployed with the U.S.S. Midway, an aircraft carrier homeported in Japan."

"That meant that you were closer to your wife, right?"

"A miss is as good as a mile," I began, "In fact it was three months after my transfer that I was able to see her again. There was a time during that three months when we pulled into port at Subic and anchored off shore, but I was not given liberty. I could see the barrio lights, where she lived scarcely a mile away, and I was tempted to jump ship and swim, but disobedience was not my nature.

Three weeks later, via a delayed Red Cross message, I learned that was the night my daughter was born."

*

The U.S.S. Midway was a floating city of five thousand, five hundred men.

Roughly four thousand made up the ship's company and crew, and the other fifteen hundred were attached to the various squadrons which comprised the Airwing.

When the ship was in port at Yokosuka I worked with my squadron which was home-ported in Atsugi. When the ship was underway I was assigned T.A.D. (Temporary Additional Duty) to the Airwing Commander's Office.

The Airwing Commander, or "Cag," presided over the squadrons, and his staff although small, was made up of revered pilots and Vietnam aces, some of the finest men I have ever known.

In charge of the enlisted men on the staff was a Senior Chief Yeoman, a slave driver, who expected eighteen hours of work each day, seven days a week, out of everyone under him.

Scuttlebutt (rumors) had it that the enlisted men had pitched in and hired contract assassins in the Philippines and Thailand to rid them of the Senior Chief, but the Chief, aware of the rumors, never ventured off the base when the ship was in port.

I was able to escape the Senior Chief's clutches much of the time by enrolling in the ship's boxing program. The Airwing Commander and his staff were proud to have a representative in the competition, and they supported me heartily, much to the Senior Chief's chagrin.

I did very well in the smokers, winning all of my fights by TKO. Before long, they were unable to find opponents willing to fight me.

They flew one guy in from another ship, a wiry black man, and former golden gloves champ. He danced like Mohamed Ally, and stung like a bee. I thought he had me in the first round, but I got lucky, cornering him, and breaking his nose in the second.

My official boxing name was "Bad news Welch," although those who betted against me referred to me as a sucker puncher, but the rest of the ship seemed to know me as "Killa'," a name I didn't like for obvious reasons.

The Midway, or "The Bird Farm" as we called her, was an old ship. Her hull was laid for a battle ship in 1941, but for whatever reasons she became an aircraft carrier instead. She was reportedly leaking through the screws, polluting the Western Pacific, and the South China Sea to the tune

83

of fifty thousand gallons of oil per week, and yet she was not scheduled for drydock repairs for several more years.

Because of the Status of Forces agreement with Japan the Midway could not remain in port in excess of twenty days over a two month period. This was because the Japanese Government felt that the ship presented a bombing risk in the case that war should break out between the U.S. and the U.S.S.R. Therefore she became the most forward deployed carrier in the Navy, and the morale of the men who sailed with her suffered for it.

After several months aboard ship, I drew two weeks leave and flew to the Philippines where I met my daughter for the first time, she was three months old, and the most beautiful little person I had ever seen. Seeing Carmen again was wonderful as well, although the precious moments shared together that I longed for were now shared with our daughter. I had missed that essential nine month transition period that prepares a couple to become a family and it saddened me.

My two weeks of heaven passed far too soon, and when it ended I found myself back at sea lonelier than ever.

The ship made brief stops in Hong Kong, Singapore, Thailand, Taiwan, Iran, Pakistan, Korea, and Australia, as well as the Philippines.

Rumor had it that the brevity of our visits was because of the crew's bad reputation for fights and raucous behavior. We all maintained that if we were allowed more time in port we wouldn't have behaved so badly.

We anchored off shore near Karachi Pakistan. The weather was hot and balmy. The liberty launch that ferried service men ashore was not nearly as full as it had been in other ports, and I surmised, before setting foot on dry land, that Pakistan was not a dream destination. My suspicions were confirmed the moment I stepped onto the dock where I was met by a group of camel jockeys, all vying for my patronage.

They tugged my arms with sweaty hands, pulling me toward their camels which were neatly leashed in a row. I tried politely to decline, but they wouldn't listen. One of the camels spat a large glob of colloidal green slobber onto the front of my dress whites and I, in a rage, forcefully broke free from their clutches, jerking and shouting obscenities. I even called the camel a son-of-a-bitch!

I decided to walk from the port, and soon found myself passing through market places where merchants sold hand crafted articles of hammered brass, polished marble, and taxidermy cobras locked in mortal combat with a stuffed mongoose.

Beggars, blind, and maimed, were everywhere. No women were to be seen, only men. The air, filled with flies, carried the stench of smoke, decay and human excrement, and I was almost compelled to return to the ship when I ran into two members of my own squadron. We shared our impressions of Pakistan as we walked together, "bazaar" was the word we agreed on.

As we passed through the city square the call to prayer rang out, and the nationals, by the hundreds, bowed on their prayer rugs. My friends also bowed, but I remained standing. "You'd better bow," they told me, "because these people will kill you."

"I bow only to Jesus Christ," I said, recalling some almost forgotten Sunday school lesson, but when I realized that every hate-filled eye was on me, I turned and hurried into an open building where I paused until the call to prayer ended before walking calmly out the other side.

I was headed back toward the docks when I came upon a group of seven U. S. Sailors clad in dress whites, standing in a half circle.

A Pakistani National sat cross-legged on the ground facing them. Beside him was a covered wicker basket three foot tall. On the ground around him were several gunny sacks, tied at the end. One of them was moving as if there was something alive inside.

I walked over and joined the sailors who were haggling with the Pakistani over price.

"Three dollars, no more!" one of the sailors held up three fingers, his voice carried a tone of finality.

Sam Welch

"Five dollars!" The Pakistani flashed his hand almost angrily, showing five fingers.

"Three!" the sailor insisted.

"Five dollars!" The Pakistani flashed his fingers again.

"We're deadlocked here," one sailor said, looking at another, and adding, "Give him five bucks Joe, I'll pay you back on payday."

"Alright," Joe said with a sigh, as he pulled out his wallet and handed the Pakistani a five dollar bill.

The Pakistani opened the wicker basket which was so full of large snakes that it was impossible to see where one began and another ended. Reaching into the basket, the Pakistani selected and gently pulled one of the snakes out and set it on the ground in front of us. The snake was at least eight feet long, and seemed fairly docile until the Pakistani slapped it on the back of the head. The snake rose up vertical, its head contorting into a hood. Swaying from side to side, it watched, challenging each one of us to step forward, its every breath a strange growl.

The Pakistani opened a gunny sack and carefully removed a mongoose, a rodent not much bigger than a rat, which he set on the ground behind the snake. The snake quickly turned its attention from us to the mongoose.

The mongoose sniffed the ground, seemingly unaware of the snake, which hovered over it. At one point the mongoose turned and rose onto his back haunches, touching noses with the snake. I couldn't help being reminded of the customary glove touch before a boxing bout.

The mongoose resumed sniffing the ground, paying little, if any attention to the snake. The snake rose higher, readying itself to strike, telegraphing its intentions twice before suddenly committing and hurling itself at the mongoose with the speed of a whip. With lightning reflexes the mongoose squealed and sprang from the would-be clutches of the snake's fangs allowing the snake no more than a mouthful of Pakistani dust.

Before the snake could recoil, the mongoose mounted the snake's back, pinning it to the ground, gnarling, and shaking the snake's head with its own razor sharp teeth, and then releasing it.

Severely wounded, the snake began striking blindly, randomly, and in that rare vortex when irony and bad luck intersect the snake's fangs found Joe's leg just above the ankle, and held fast.

Joe screamed in a voice an octave above the average male, "Get it off! Get it off!"

While the rest of us watched in shock and disbelief the Pakistani grabbed the snake's tail and tugged on it like a rope. Joe fell backwards to the ground half screaming, half crying, "I'm gonna' die, I'm gonna' die!"

Releasing Joe's ankle, the snake whipped around and latched onto the Pakistani's forearm. The Pakistani squeezed the snake's jaws with his free hand and carefully worked the fangs from his arm. Once free he held the thrashing snake by the head while he found an empty gunny sack with his other arm and stuffed it inside. After tying the top of the sack, he tossed it onto the ground where it flip-flopped from side to side and end over end.

Joe continued to cry and wheeze, "I'm gonna' die!" His friends had cut his pant leg with a pocket knife, and were about to lance the wound in order to suck out the venom when one of them looked at the other and exclaimed, "Not me dude, I got cavities!"

"How about you?" One of them asked, pointing at me.

Instinctively my hand covered my mouth, and I nodded as I heard myself say, "Cavities-cavities!"

The Pakistani who was wiping the blood from the puncture wounds in his arm, looked up and motioned to the sailors. "It's okay!" he calmed.

I walked away wondering if the Pakistani was trying to tell us that the venom had been milked from the snake.

After the ship pulled out I asked the flight surgeon if he knew anything about the incident. He said that he was unaware of any snake-bite victims, and he suggested that the sailor I described was probably from one of the other ships in our carrier group.

Sam Welch

*

Shellie sat spellbound, almost mesmerized by the story. I waved my hand in front of her face. "Wake up Shellie."

It took her a moment to come around. I wasn't surprised since that story had the same effect on other women, and I was often prompted by a friend who brought a different girl every Saturday night to a weekly dinner date. He always seated his latest date between us, and after dinner he'd mention Pakistan, adding, "You were in Pakistan weren't you Sam?" and that was my cue.

When I reached the part where the snake was about to strike, I would cup my hand like a cobra moving slowly in hypnotic fashion in front of my friend's unsuspecting dinner date. With my other hand I grabbed her knee under the table. The knee grabbing incited spontaneous screaming, and even fainting on more than one occasion. I found myself wondering if this was what God meant in Genesis 3:15 when he told the serpent, "I will put enmity between you and the woman."

My story became a weekly ritual prompting cooks, waitresses, and regulars to break from whatever they were doing and watch. It was their, "Quick, Sam's telling that snake story again"—break. We had to ask them to be as inconspicuous as possible because a sudden audience made the girls suspicious.

"Wow!" Shellie shook her head slightly while rolling her eyes. "Poor Joe!"

I shook my head in agreement, and drew a breath between clenched teeth, feigning as much concern as I could muster. "Yes! Poor Joe!" *Regardless of his fate he never had a clue how much entertainment his five dollars inspired.*

"Okay, tell me more." Shellie leaned forward, fully recovered from my snake story.

"This isn't fair," I protested, "it's all been about me. You haven't told me anything about you!"

"We'll get to that after you're done with your story, after-all, you've only caught me up on four years, you've got fifteen more to go." I drew an exaggerated sigh and continued.

Chapter Thirteen

In the months that followed I grew so disenchanted with shipboard life that I wrote a letter to President Carter citing the amount of oil that was leaking through the ship's screws. I also enclosed a Filipino newspaper clipping containing a statement made by the U.S. Ambassador to the Philippines, concerning the renegotiations of the rental agreement for the military bases in the Philippines. According to the Philippine newspapers, the U.S. Ambassador had told President Marcos that the American people could afford more money for the bases. When I read this I was infuriated. *Who was he to throw around America's tax dollars as though it didn't matter?*

The U.S. bases served to protect the Philippines, and the U.S. Ambassador should have America's best interest at heart rather than his own.

A month later it was announced that the USS Midway was to undergo an unscheduled dry-dock repair in Yokosuka. I also learned that the U.S. Ambassador to the Philippines had been replaced.

My first thought on the two matters was *what an amazing coincidence,* but then I discovered I had been written up for bypassing the chain of command, and that I would have to face a Captain's Mast (a form of military trial).

Before the Captain's Mast convened I received an official letter from Joseph Hidalgo, the Undersecretary of the Navy, thanking me on behalf of President Carter for bringing these matters to his attention.

In light of the President's gratitude the charges against me were promptly dropped, and I, along with the rest of the crew, enjoyed a two month stay in port.

During that time I brought Carmen and our child Ilene to Japan. We rented a house outside the Naval base in a suburb known as Honshu. It was a small house with paper walls, matted bamboo floors and a benjo toilet. We huddled around kerosene heaters to keep warm during the cold Japanese winter months, and slept wrapped in warm silk Korean blankets on Japanese futon mattresses.

Carmen remained with me in Japan until she became pregnant with our second child and then she returned to the Philippines to have the baby.

When the time came to transfer from the USS Midway, I received orders to report to embassy duty in Iran. I knew that Iran was a hotbed of hatred for Americans, and that it was only a matter of time before U.S. relations with Iran broke down completely. When I refused the orders I was once again threatened with Captain's Mast.

I called my detailer in New Orleans, the guy who issues orders. He told me that my name was on a blacklist in Washington D.C., that I was considered a trouble maker, for writing letters to the wrong people.

"Blacklisters are commonly sent to embassy duty in harms' way, but you didn't hear this from me," he said.

I stood firm on my refusal of the orders, knowing I had only five months left on my enlistment, and even if I got busted in rank I would soon be a happy civilian anyway.

A few weeks before my transfer date my detailer had a change of heart and offered me shore duty at Mare Island Naval Station in Vallejo, California. The only catch was I had to extend my enlistment for two additional years. Charges against me were again dropped, and I was transferred to Mare Island where I was able to live with my wife and our two daughters.

Refusing the orders for embassy duty in Iran turned out to be a good choice. Shortly after my transfer date the embassy was overrun by militant Islamists, and the embassy personnel were held hostage for four-hundred, forty-four days.

Settling into a normal lifestyle was a difficult transition. Something was missing in my life, and the bullshit from the previous four years weighed heavily upon me.

Sam Welch

I began reading, studying my Bible, searching for answers to a question that I could not even define. I read 1st John 3:9 "Any man born of God cannot continue to sin because God's seed is in him," and like a festering wound breaks open, I broke.

It was a Wednesday night, and I found my way to a boring, halfhearted, Bible study at the local Assemblies of God Church.

During the closing prayer I realized that if something didn't happen immediately, I would walk away the same way I came in, desperate for help, and unfulfilled.

Interrupting the closing prayer, I shouted, "Wait! I need help!"

The pastor seemed a little offended when he asked, "What seems to be the problem here?" The people attending the meeting, perhaps forty in all, were shocked as well.

I can't say I wasn't embarrassed, but I forced out, "I've never been able to stop sinning, I want to be born of God, and although I am sorry for interrupting your meeting, I can't let this moment pass. I can't walk out of here the same as when I came in!"

The Pastor's voice softened, "Come forward," he said, motioning with his hand.

As I made my way to the front, he called for people to gather around me and pray. When they prayed my world began to spin around me, slowly at first, and then rapidly. It was a wonderful feeling, as the weight of the world was lifted from my shoulders. Tears flowed from my eyes, and happiness like I had never known filled my inner being. I knew I was born again.

In the days and weeks that followed, I couldn't stop talking about it. I lost all my old friends. They avoided me like a plague. I attended church every time the doors opened, but I was so ablaze that even the old church members shied away from me. I studied the scriptures, which had suddenly come alive to me, incessantly. I was not just saved, I was radically saved!

About three weeks after my conversion I had an amazing dream, a dream more vivid than any I have had before; I was seated in a church in the front row on the right hand side. There were people seated behind me, scattered

92

about on the benches. We were all facing the stage and a pulpit, waiting for the service which seemed long overdue. I was overwhelmed with an annoying impatience, and when I could tolerate it no longer I stood to my feet, raised my hands and began to shout praises to God.

I could feel the ridicule from the people seated behind me, and the overwhelming pressure demanding that I sit down and shut up, but I determined that I would stand and continue to worship with all my heart and strength regardless of what they thought.

One by one they stood and joined me in worship, praising God aloud.

A voice somewhere behind me called out the words, "Jesu Soriana," and I wondered what it meant. Again I heard the same words from above the crowd and I looked about to see where it came from.

While I stood mystified, the words went from merely spoken to being repeated in song by the most beautiful voices in differing tones and harmony, first from one direction, and then another with timing beyond human calculation.

The most beautiful sound I have ever heard remained a mystery to me until a voice said, "This means Jesus is coming!" The words, "Jesus is coming," filled me with joy and inspired me to praise God from the depths of my being. Instantly we, the worshippers were all swept into the air. I dreamt I was flying and as I awakened I felt as if I dropped into my mattress. Fully conscious, I continued worshipping God, and wondering at this strange dream.

*

"So you think the dream had meaning?" Shellie remained expressionless, hard to read.

"I think it represents my calling. I'm called to make a stand for the Lord, and because of my stand others will stand as well." I replied.

She seemed as unaffected by my reply as she had been with my story. Whatever her thoughts were on the matter she kept them to herself. I, in turn, dismissed my concerns. I had long since learned not to care whether friends or co-workers deemed me rational or insane, and so it came as a funny-you-should-ask moment when she posed the question, "so what have you been doing for work these past years?"

Chapter Fourteen

After my enlistment expired in March of 1981 I was honorably discharged, and we moved to Brookings in Southern Oregon where I had spent most of my youth. My house had fallen into disrepair and had been condemned. Thieves had taken everything of value. The windows were all broken, the doors were torn off, and the words "helter skelter" had been spray painted on the walls.

Compounding matters, the city had bancrofted a new sewer line in the area, and assessed a lien on the property in the amount of $8,500.

Jobs were few and far between. I worked part-time for minimum wage, wherever and whenever I could.

A developer made an offer on my property. The offer was low, but I was desperate.

With the down payment we purchased an old mobile home, and moved into a mobile home park. It wasn't much, but it was a place to live.

I got a job with a car dealership where I worked for about a year. After that I worked for a fabrication shop where I learned to weld and cut metals.

In September 1982 our third child, Michael was born, and with the added responsibility I became aware that I needed to further my education in order to get a better paying job.

In 1983 we moved to Woodville. I worked at a stud mill for minimum wage during the day, making one hundred, twenty dollars a week, and I attended classes at a community college at night.

When Carmen became pregnant again we had no idea how we would afford it, but the only option we ever considered was that our family would grow, and if we had to be poor then we would endure it.

We continued to struggle, and when we missed our third car payment we received a legal notice telling us our car was going to be repossessed.

Sam Welch

There is an old saying, "there are no atheists in fox holes," and although I wasn't an atheist, I found myself in dire need of a rescue, and as such I began to cry out to God and to search my Bible for answers. I came upon the scripture, "Will a man rob God? Yet you rob me. But you ask, "How do we rob you?"

"In tithes and offerings. You are under a curse—the whole nation of you—because you are robbing me. Bring the whole tithe into the storehouse, that there may be food in my house. Test me in this," says the Lord Almighty, "and see if I will not throw open the floodgates of heaven and pour out so much blessing that you will not have room enough for it."
Malachi 3:8-10

I didn't have enough money to tithe, and giving money away when I was nearly starving made no sense at all, but a slogan from an old evangelist kept ringing in my ear, "Let God be true, and every man a liar!"

I didn't have much to lose, I only made $120 per week, and the following payday when I handed Carmen $108, having deducted $12 for tithe, she nearly went through the roof.

"Did you get a pay cut? What happened to the other twelve dollars?"
"I tithed it!" I replied.

"You mean you gave it to the church?" Her voice was somewhat cynical, laced with fury along with a touch of resentment.

I nodded, trying to conceal my sheepish tendencies, and stand firm, while every impulse told me to run and hide.

She broke into a crying-screaming frenzy, "How could you do that when they're about to take our car, and we can't even make the rent payment, let alone put enough food on the table to feed our kids!" I knew where she was coming from as she continued to rant, and I listened wishing
I could hold her and say, "Everything will be alright." At the same time

96

I realized that we were on a floundering ship, spiraling into a massive whirlpool, and if God didn't lift us out we would certainly go under.

She packed her bags and loaded them into the car. My heart sank within my chest as she started the engine and began to back away without so much as a "Goodbye." Moments later she pulled back into the carport and shut off the engine. Her sobs carried through the bedroom window as I lay on my bed unable to sleep.

At three A.M. she came back inside and laid down on the bed opposite me. "I'd leave you Sammy, but there's no gas in the car!" she said in a "you'd better believe it!" tone.

*

We couldn't afford a hospital birth, or a doctor, but a local midwife accepted Carmen as her patient. Her overall fee, including delivery was $700.

I took on some part-time work in addition to school and my regular minimum wage job. I was able to scrounge $353.53 for the midwife.

Meanwhile, aware that our car was to be repossessed, Carmen took the car back to the credit union in Brookings. The plan was to give them the car and catch a bus home.

The loan officer would not accept the keys, but instead offered Carmen a two month payment extension, and sent her home with the car.

As the day of our child's birth neared we went for our scheduled midwife appointment. After Carmen entered the examination room, leaving me alone with the midwife, the midwife turned to me. Grabbing my collar she growled, "You still owe three hundred forty seven dollars and forty seven cents, and if you don't have it by the time your wife gives birth, she can have that baby out in the street!" The midwife pointed toward the window and added, "If you think I'm joking just try me!"

The two remaining weeks of Carmen's final trimester passed, and I was unable to raise or borrow the balance. The days narrowed to hours with no solution in sight, until scarcely an hour before Carmen's labor when I opened the mailbox and found a kicker check from the State of

Oregon, a "renter's refund" in the amount of three hundred forty seven dollars and forty seven cents. I had to control myself to keep from stepping in front of passing cars.

That afternoon Carmen gave birth to a perfect baby boy, "Justice!"

A few months later we learned that our midwife had been caught in a sting. She had conspired with an undercover deputy posing as a hit-man in a plot to murder her step daughter over a life insurance policy. She was eventually convicted and sentenced for the crime.

*

When our oldest son, Michael was two years old, one of the neighbor kids got a new pet, a baby duckling. The duckling was the cutest thing I've ever seen. From its soft down, and its high pitched peep, to the way it scampered awkwardly, gobbling sow bugs, which ran for their lives when boards were overturned. I don't know why, but I found myself visualizing it from the bug's point of view and thinking of a Japanese Godzilla movie.

Michael was enamored with the duckling, and begged me constantly to buy one for him. I would have, but I was afraid he would affectionately smother it, and besides, I was far too concerned with making a living to be bothered with trivial matters.

I learned that a dryer was being installed at the local veneer plant, and the plant was going to hire twelve new people. The job was expected to pay nine dollars an hour which was more than twice what I was making at minimum wage. I submitted an application, and every night and morning I prayed, begging God for the job.

One morning I awakened from a dream. In the dream I was a two year old child standing in front of my father, God. In each of his hands he held a baby duckling. As he extended his hand with one of the ducklings I anxiously stepped forward to grab it, but then a sobering thought awakened me. The child—me, was likely to smother that duckling.

That morning the superintendent from the veneer plant called to say that I had been hired.

I began my new job as Dryer Puller on swing shift. The job was easy when the dryer ran at its normal pace, but a new set of controls had been installed, and the dryer could be sped up or slowed by buttons on the electrical panel.

The Superintendent was a short man rumored to have the Napoleon complex. The guys referred to him, outside of his hearing, as "The Little Shit."

Each day when my shift began the Superintendent accelerated the dryer to the point where it spat out wet veneer onto the huge, steel offbearer table faster than I could pull and stack it.

Afterward the little shit would pace back and forth on the catwalk overlooking the table, shaking his head while I worked feverishly in a futile effort to catch up.

When I asked the Dryer Tender what was going on he explained that the little shit knew a girl that he wanted to hire, and that he was trying to make an opening for her. Since he needed justification for letting me go, he was speeding up the dryer to prove that I wasn't capable of doing the job. "Nothing personal," the dryer tender added, as if corrupt motives validated any objective.

Realizing that my three week trial period was about to end, I was overwhelmed with the fear of having to accept that I wasn't good enough.

I struggled with the thought of working for minimum wage, and the poverty that I had fought so hard to escape. How would I explain to my wife that I had failed?

I found myself unable to eat or sleep. Realizing that I was like the child smothering the duckling, I prayed for guidance, but it seemed as if God was silent.

Tuesday of what was to be my final week, the little shit sped up the dryer, filling the table with more wet veneer than I could sort and pull. He walked away shaking his head, stopping briefly for a word with the Dryer Tender before leaving.

Sam Welch

Moments later as the Dryer Tender helped me catch up, I asked what the Super had said.

"He said, 'Thursday will be your last day!'" the Dryer Tender replied.

The words resounded in my mind throughout the shift, hampering my thoughts, and sapping my strength.

I had two choices, I could wait it out and be fired, or I could quit. I decided on the latter.

The following morning I went with a heavy heart to the little shit's office to set the duckling free.

He invited me in and motioned to a chair in front of his desk. I sat down, having rehearsed every word at least a hundred times.

"What's on your mind?" He growled with the tone of a man who has the world by the tail and is keenly aware of it.

"Well, I..." a lump filled my throat. I swallowed, and began again, "I..." A third time I cleared and tried to speak, but tears formed in my eyes, and pressure in my sinuses. That un-suppressible pain that precedes tears, rendering me unable to speak. I shook my head and raised a, "please give me a moment" finger.

As if it wasn't humiliating enough being at the mercy of this little bully, I now found myself crying in front of him.

He took a box of clean-exes from his desk and pushed them toward me. After a deep, hard-released sigh, he threw his hands up and began, "What's the matter with you, why can't you do the work? You look strong enough, is it just a lack of coordination?

I tried to gulp and regain my speech but the lump in my throat proved too hard to swallow.

"Wait a minute!" As if a light had dawned in his mind, "You came in here to quit, that's why you came in here, you came here to quit, didn't you?"

I nodded, drying my eyes with my second and third clean-exe, folded together, and then I forced, "I-I really needed this job, but I'd rather quit than be fired. I've gotten to the point where I can't eat or sleep."

He sighed again and dropped his head, a look of remorse on his face. "Well don't quit just yet. I'll give you three more weeks of probation, just show me that you really want the job. Come in a half hour early each day, and work with the day-shift off-bearer, soak up all the pointers you can get from him and we'll see what happens. Meanwhile, go home and have Momma cook ya' a big steak."

I grabbed a few more clean-exes and walked from the office to the parking lot, my eyes still filled with tears, but they were tears of joy and gratitude to God, because I knew that the duckling-job was mine, and that no man could take it from me. I was still drying my eyes when I collided with the back window of a Chevy Blazer. I found myself face to face with a bumper sticker. The picture showed Elmer Fud with a shotgun chasing Daffy Duck. The caption read, "If you love something set it free. If it doesn't come back, hunt it down and kill it!"

"Oh God," I cried out, "sometimes you are so funny!"

*

"I fail to see the humor in that!" Shellie's expression remained solemn.

"Really?"

She nodded from side to side, allowing a sudden smile. "Of course not really, silly! Can't you tell when I'm joking? I love your stories! I could sit here all day and listen." She paused and sipped her coke, and after a quick swallow asked, "So did the Superintendent, I mean the little shit ever hire the girl?"

"Yes he did, but her attendance was so bad that they had to fire her. She filed a sexual harassment suit against him, I think it was settled out of court."

Shellie chuckled. "It's funny how karma is sometimes just the obvious, you-can-see-it-comin', result of pure stupidity."

"Yes, that's true," I agreed, adding, "and to tack insult to the little shit's injury, the mill electrician disconnected the buttons in the control box. The little shit continued to play with the controls daily, but it had no effect on the dryer. I don't think he ever figured it out either."

Shellie laughed heartily, and I joined with a chuckle. The waitress approached and stood quietly looking at us, obviously shy about interrupting. I nodded to let her know she had my attention.

"Our breakfast menu ends in twenty minutes, and I'm going on my break in five. If you want breakfast you should order now, otherwise, if you prefer lunch you can catch me after break."

"I'm not hungry right now, thank you." I nodded toward Shellie.

"You?" Shellie looked up at the waitress. "Neither am I, but we'll have another
Coke when you return from your break."

I felt bad *about* not ordering food, but the refills weren't free so *whatthe-heck! It couldn't hurt to stay and chat a little longer, besides I hadn't heard her story.* I looked at Shellie, "so tell me about you."

"You haven't finished telling me about the mill!" Her statement seemed part objection, part complaint with a touch of impatience mixed in.

I pondered the years that followed, years of uneventful joy, the joy of working without worry and watching my children grow, years unworthy of a story.

"Well, I went from dryer to greenchain, and from there to a utility position. My job description as a utility worker included unclogging the lilly-pad chipper, which chipped up the large rounds cut from the ends of logs. My other duties included feeding cull logs to the splitter operator, and filling in for him during his breaks. I frequently unclogged the mill chipper, and pulled greenchain when it suited the foreman, and it suited him often.

"Everything was great for a while, and then one day God spoke to me."

Chapter Fifteen

"Chuck's brother is going to join anachronism!" the voice was soft and masculine, nearly arousing me from a sound sleep. "I don't understand!" I mumbled, hazily aware of my own reply, yet too drowsy to be concerned with the subject matter, or that someone was talking to me in my bedroom when I thought I was alone.

It's a bad organization!"

Once again I almost awoke, acknowledging the statement with an, "Uhha!" before nodding back to sleep.

"Chuck's brother is going to join anachronism!" the voice repeated, in the same tone as the earlier statement.

"I don't know what that means," I replied, this time I awakened alarmed at the realization that someone had entered my bedroom without my knowledge and was carrying on a conversation with me.

"It's a bad organization!" he repeated.

I rolled over briskly to see who was speaking to me, but there was no one there.

Springing from my bed in the realization that this was a message, perhaps from God, which carried some urgency, I searched shelves and countertops for a pen while repeating the word "anachronism." I found a pencil and an envelope, but as I began to write the lead broke. I continued to search in vain for a pen in the dim morning light through sleepy eyes. Finally satisfied, having spoken the word at least a hundred times, that I would remember it even if I resumed my sleep, I took a leak, downed a glass of water, and returned to bed.

I awakened several hours later, having forgotten the word 'anachronism,' although it was on the tip of my tongue. I recalled merely that Chuck's brother was going to join a bad organization.

Sam Welch

I knew only one person named Chuck. He was a well-liked young man who worked with me in the mill. I knew his brother as well, in fact I knew Jeff by name, that's why the message didn't seem to make sense. God, at least I assumed it was God, knows Jeff's name, and therefore the message became a mystery. Was he really referring to Jeff?

That afternoon when I arrived for my shift I found a notice on the time clock informing all employees of pay-scale adjustments. The new pay-scale, effective almost immediately, lowered the hourly wage for almost every position in the mill to an average wage supposedly compiled from similar jobs in other mills. Naturally the white collar, six figure nobility in management assumed they could easily sell pay cuts to the less intelligent, lower echelon millworkers if they candy coated their intentions with a label like "pay adjustments."

They were wrong, the men were livid, and everyone spoke of unionizing.

That evening the Swing-shift Foreman sent me to help out on the greenchain. I was working across from Chuck, and when I found the opportunity I reluctantly, and not without reservations, shared the message to which I had awakened that morning. Chuck was somewhat of a Christian, and since it concerned only him and his brother I asked him not to let anyone else in on it.

"That's just like Jeff," said Chuck, "he joins every organization that comes along."

Moments later the lathe broke down, and the rest of the greenchain crew gathered around Chuck to discuss the pay cuts and the union.

"When we unionize," said one, "we'll be a brotherhood, a band of brothers united in our cause. We'll teach management a lesson they'll never forget!"

"I don't know who'd want to be Chuck's brother," blurted another, inspiring a round of laughter from the group.

The words struck a strange chord with me, and I found myself wondering if "Chuck's brother" referred to the millworkers rather than Jeff, and if the "bad organization" was really the union.

The men beamed their support for the union with raised fists, reminding me of a bar scene from an old black-and-white "Three Musketeers" movie. For a moment I likened them to the beer-crazed, feather hatted cavaliers with raised swords, rallying, "all for one, and one for all." I could almost see them mounting and riding away, hell-bent on conquest—a conquest cut short as the repaired lathe sent steaming veneer careening down the greenchain, and the men hurrying back to their work stations.

*

In the weeks that followed the men voted overwhelmingly 82-2, to unionize, and every man was required to fill out a pledge card affirming their allegiance to the union. Even the Seventh Day Adventists within the crew, who are not required to join because of religious objections, waved their exemption and joined wholeheartedly.

Because of my reservations I held back, refusing to sign, although I was still uncertain that the union was the anachronism, the "bad organization."

The sentiment of the workers increasingly turned against me. I became known as "that fucking scab who hears voices and thinks God talks to him," and I realized Chuck had betrayed my confidence."

I never confronted Chuck about the matter, I needed all the friends I could get, and when I learned that he had a 1976 Ford Granada for sale I dropped by his house to take a look.

"It has a bad transmission," he said, "but the engine runs good.

I needed a car for my daughter, who had recently got her license. I could easily change a transmission, and the price was right, so we struck up a deal.

I asked Chuck if I could change the transmission at his house. He agreed, and while I was changing the tranny Chuck's brother, Jeff offered to help. I couldn't turn down good help, and while we worked together under the car I took the opportunity to warn him about joining a bad organization.

"I've joined ten organizations in the past year. I'm the president of one, vice president of three, and a card carrying member in the rest." He chuckled and continued with, "recently I joined a crazy organization where we have sword fights with cardboard swords, and joust with fake lances. It's a hoot!"

"Really! What's it called?" I couldn't help but wonder what kind of enjoyment people get from fighting with cardboard swords.

"It's the Society for something or other, some big word that I can't even pronounce, but duels aren't even the half of it. They set up medieval tent cities on the weekend, and everyone gets to leave the hectic grind of the real world and become someone else." "Wow!"

"We've got kings, queens, dukes, ladies in waiting, squires, and naves! You name it, we've got it! The interesting thing is our king is just a deck hand in the real world. The queen is some attorney's wife, but she sleeps with our deckhand king, and her real husband, the attorney is just a nave!" He broke into laughter and wiped his mouth with the sleeve of his sweatshirt being careful not to touch his face with his greasy wrist.

"You mean, they sleep together?" I nearly dropped my wrench.

"Yep! Everybody knows about it. Most of the members like to think that this medieval life is their reality, while their real life is just a fantasy, and just cuz you're married in the real world doesn't mean you're married in our world!"

"That doesn't sound like a very good organization to me." I told him, wondering that people could have no sense of the consequences such a lifestyle could cause.

I finished the car on a weekend and returned to work feeling less confident than ever that the message I had received had anything to do with the union, but I postponed joining because I wasn't sure.

I continued to be the brunt of jokes and angry sentiment. The men needed someone to hate, and I was that someone. Their hatred for me grew and in addition to the insults, my truck was often vandalized in the parking lot.

My wife began receiving threats over the phone from men claiming that they were going to kill her and the kids. She also received calls from wives of other millworkers telling her what an idiot she had for a husband. In her mind it was all my fault for not joining the union, and I found myself almost as uncomfortable at home as I was at work. To make matters worse I overheard some of my co-workers joking that my wife was about to leave me, and it disturbed me that they enjoyed meddling in my personal matters.

The Union President contacted the pastor of the local church which I attended, and discovered that the Assemblies of God had nothing in its by-laws that kept its members from joining unions. He also discovered that I had never filled out a church membership card, which caused him to conclude that I had no religious grounds for not joining the union. He then contacted the management of the mill and demanded that they set a date by which I would either join the union or be terminated. The management agreed, and I was given a "join or be fired" ultimatum.

I put the matter to serious prayer, but as the deadline approached I received no answer from God, besides it was never made clear to me by God whether I was or was not supposed to join this bad organization, and so I agreed that I would sign on the day of the deadline.

When the deadline rolled around the Shop Steward met me in the break room. He opened his briefcase but was unable to find the pledge card which he swore had been there earlier. "No matter," he said, "I'll meet you here same time same place tomorrow, and I'll cover for you."

That night I dreamt I was the groom in a wedding ceremony. Standing next to me was a veiled bride, whom I could only see from the corner of my eye. The preacher, gruff and demanding bellowed out, "Do you, Sam take this man to be your lawful wedded wife?"

In shock I glanced to my right. Thru the bride's veil I could see a man's face with a dark three day beard. I was appalled! Everything within me wanted to cry out, "NO!"

Again came the preacher's voice, his tone even more demanding, "Do you, Sam, take this man to be your lawful wedded wife?"

I heard behind me a crowd heckling me and demanding my answer. As I half turned I realized that my audience were my 83 co-workers.

Reluctantly, and only because of peer pressure, I opened my mouth intending to say, "I do," but a voice interrupted, booming down from above me, "**Understand, you don't have to do this!**"

The noise and vibration of the voice shook me upright in my bed, and there I sat in a cold sweat thanking God for his answer, and praising him as well because the wedding, that had seemed so real, was only a dream.

The following day I met the Shop Steward in the break room. He held up the pledge card. "I'm sorry for the inconvenience..."

"I've changed my mind," I interrupted, "I'm not joining after-all!"

An expression of rage formed on his face. "I bent over backwards to cover for you, and this is what I get!" he blurted.

"Yep, but thanks for your efforts!"

"Did God talk to you again, or something?" His voice reeked of ridicule.

It didn't deserve a response, but responding wouldn't make matters worse, so I nodded as I walked out, and offered, "he said 'I don't have to do it!'"

"You'll get fired!" he shouted with a forced laugh.

I stopped and turned. "Maybe so, but I don't have to do it!"

A few days later two of my so-called Christian co-workers paid me a visit at home. They seemed very concerned about my wellbeing, and I knew that their real concern was my state of mental health, after-all, everyone knows that God doesn't really talk to people, and paying a confused friend a visit was the Christian thing to do. *How could Sam not see that he was being deceived?*

The proverbial cat was already out of the bag, so I shared with them my most recent dream: I was walking in my yard looking at the winter grass, sparse and patchy. I was told I had to go away for a while. When I returned the grass was luscious and green like spring grass. I heard a voice say, "Let your neighbor mow your grass," and then I saw a man coming from the neighbor's yard to mow my grass. The man was moderate height, his hair short, and blondish. He was stocky and well dressed, with a shirt and tie, and dress shoes—not by any means grass mowing attire. As he entered my yard I awakened.

I explained to my bewildered friends that I understood from the dream that I would be fired, but that I would return to my job in the spring. They seemed amused at my interpretation, and asked me what was meant by "Let your neighbor mow your grass." I had to confess that I didn't know, but that I was sure to find out in due time.

When they left I could tell that their visit had only enhanced their suspicions that I was crazy. I wish I could have let it roll off my shoulders, but I laid awake praying and crying out to God. I told him, "I feel like the man who had the talking horse. He boasted about his horse, but when his friends came to hear the horse talk, the horse remained silent, making him seem like a fool. Why, Lord have you revealed yourself to me, but you won't reveal yourself to my friends?"

The following morning, Carmen awakened me. "I had the strangest dream!" she said.

"Tell me your dream," I told her.

"I dreamt I had the most beautiful doll! The doll could talk, and it was intelligent beyond words." She paused for a moment, a moment that lingered beyond my tolerance.

I sat up in bed, my heart beating anxiously in my chest. "Yes, yes?"

"I called all my friends to come and see my doll, and hear it talk." Again she paused, yawning and stretching.

"And what happened? What happened?"

She shot me an angry glance from the corner of her eye that told me she was annoyed with my impatience.

"Well, what happened?" I persisted.

With a sigh of disgust she continued, "All my friends came, but the doll wouldn't talk to them! It just sat there like a dumb doll. After they left, making fun of me, and thinking I was crazy, I turned to the doll, and I said, 'why have you revealed yourself to me, but you won't reveal yourself to my friends?'"

She paused again, and I began to choke on my own saliva. I slapped my chest once, twice, and cleared my throat. In a raspy whisper I forced, "And what did the doll say?"

"You're acting crazy!" she accused, adding, "Give me a minute!"

Unable to contain my excitement, I found myself shaking her by the shoulders, and demanding, "What did it say? What did it say?"

"Stop it!" she shouted, threatening me with a clenched right fist.

Realizing that I was a little out of control, I released her. "Okay, sorry, so what did the doll say?"

She shook her head and gave me that look of ultimate disgust. "The doll said, 'Because I don't like them!'"

*

Shellie sipped her Coke. A borderline smirk with a hint of a smile formed on her lips. "So you got fired?"

"Yep, they sent a big wig down from management to escort me out of the building. Workers watching from their work stations paused to applaud and cheer as I walked out, but that wasn't the worst of it, the shit really hit the fan when I came home unemployed. Carmen wasn't havin' it, she said she was going to leave me. Had to tell her to watch out for the door on her way out!"

Shellie chuckled. "Did she get over it?"

"Three days later I hired on at a nearby redwood plywood plant, making two dollars more per hour than I made at the Woodville plant. It was like a breath of fresh air. Working conditions were great, people treated me like a human being. There were a lot of pretty women on my shift, and they all seemed to like me."

"Shame on you!" She raised her coke to her mouth.

I shrugged. "Vanity has always been my weakness, but I never let it get out of hand." I raised a forefinger and nodded to emphasize my point.

Shellie lowered her glass quickly, and covered her mouth to hold back her drink. I could tell by her reaction the coke had gone into her nose. I handed her a napkin. "I hate when that happens," I said.

Moments passed before she recovered enough to speak. "I seem to recall hearing about an incident where an angry mother pulled a gun on you, and I'm sure your vanity was WELL in hand!"

I pretended not to catch her pun. "I don't recall telling you about that," I said, realizing that grapevine stories are often stretched out of shape.

"Well, little birds know their way around this neck of the woods. That's why I said your hindsight was thirty-thirty!"

"You're right, it was a thirty-thirty Marlin, and she came that close to blowing my head off!" I showed Shellie a one inch gap between my thumb and forefinger. "It was during the time when you broke our steady and suggested we see other people so you could go out with Dave." "Just a minute!" she protested, maintaining a perplexed smile.

"Well, you did!" I insisted.

"I guess I did," she admitted, relaxing somewhat. "You must have done something pretty serious for the girl's mother to pull a gun!"

"Not at all!" I said, wondering if this rumor had contributed to our breakup so long ago. "It was very innocent," I continued, "although Jan had a crush on me, and invited me over for a visit when her mother was gone. We were sitting under the apple tree chatting when her mother showed up with a gun. She threatened to shoot me, but agreed to give me a head start. I like to think I was better at sprinting than she was at shooting. A few years later that woman murdered all five of her kids. End of story!" I gave Shellie my best look of finality, hoping to change a bitter subject. There was no reason to expand the matter. The story served no purpose aside from setting Shellie's mind at ease and making me realize that I had hurt her as well.

I drew a deep breath and recalled our earlier conversation, "Anyway, regardless of the girls at the redwood plant, it was a great workplace. I stayed there for three and a half months."

"Why did you leave if it was so good?"

"Because I knew I was supposed to return to the Woodville plant! Remember the dream, I returned to the Spring grass?"

"Huh?"

Chapter Sixteen

A lovely springtime Sunday-go-to-church morning had dawned in Woodville, and all seemed right with the world. The irony was that I had experienced a peaceful winter even with its relentless cold rain, and intermittent snow and frost.

Despite the new birth of flowers, trees in foliage, and the beauty of the bird's song, I knew I was going back to the Woodville plant, and that all the pleasantries of spring couldn't lessen the storm that I was about to endure.

The pastor met me in the church foyer with a letter in his hand and a smile on his face. "This came in for you," he beamed, handing me the letter, adding, "well, not really for you, but it concerns your situation, and I can't help thinking that this letter is the answer to your prayers." He pointed to the return address and continued, "I called this organization and talked to one of their attorneys, he said that they would be happy to take your case for free!"

He handed me the letter and I gave it a quick glance. It was a form letter from the National Right to Work Legal Defense Foundation. Naturally it had been opened, otherwise, how would the pastor have known to call them?

"Please promise me that you will call them first thing tomorrow morning!"

"I will, I promise I'll call, and thank you." I told him.

Sunday services at the Woodville Assemblies of God Church were heart-wrenching, convicting, and soul-freeing. Not a dry eye remained at the close of the service. All-in-all it was wonderful.

Afterward came the backyard barbeque, and catch with the kids, and...

*

"Did you call them?" Shellie broke in, making me realize that she wasn't interested in Church services and back yard barbecues.

"Yes, as a matter of fact. The following morning I called the National Right to Work Legal Defense Foundation, and spoke with one of the attorneys. He said that we needed to pursue the situation through the proper channels, and that the first thing to do was to file a complaint with the Equal Employment Opportunity Commission, which was a federal government agency. The nearest office was in neighboring, Washington State. I wasted no time calling, and in less than two weeks they sent an attorney to investigate my case. He looked a lot like the man from my dream who came to mow my grass.

After the investigation the Equal Employment Opportunity Commission ruled in my favor that the union and the company had equally discriminated against me, and wrongfully terminated me. They had to offer my job back.

If I hadn't made so much money at the redwood plant, they would have been forced to pay my back wages as well, but the only thing they had to pay was the difference in mileage for my daily commute which amounted to about $1400. The mill paid half, and the Union the other half.

Shortly after the ruling I received several "you didn't hear this from me" calls from former friends and co-workers warning me that the Union vice president had called for a special meeting with the workers to inform them of my return.

According to my sources the Union V.P. told them that I had taken their hard earned union dues in an unjust settlement, and although the Union could not authorize any action against me, they could not stop the men if they wanted to take it upon themselves. His speech created quite a stir among some of the men who immediately began to plan my accidental demise. My sources were not exactly well-wishers, they were just former co-workers who were aware of the plots against me and didn't want to be a party to murder.

Almost immediately the threatening phone calls to my home phone resumed, along with former co-workers driving by my house throwing garbage into my yard and driveway, and shouting obscenities at my kids."

"Sounds like a great bunch of guys!" Shellie shook her head, obviously surprised.

"Yeah, like a pack of dogs!" I sipped my coke, swallowed and cleared my throat, pondering the events that followed.

*

The first day back at work I parked my old truck in the parking lot at the Woodville plant, knowing it would receive the same abuse and vandalism that it had received before I was fired, broken lights, scratches and dents. I couldn't help but chuckle, happy that it was an old truck, and that I would not lose sleep over every new battle scar.

As I entered the plant through the large open bay the Hyster driver spotted me. Whipping the Hyster around, he sped toward me at full throttle. I hadn't expected attempts on my life to be so blatant. For a moment I hesitated in surprise, but realizing I had mere seconds to react, I sprang behind a concrete footing like a clumsy matador abandoning all finesse and esteem to dodge a charging bull.

Missing me by inches, the Hyster screeched along the concrete creating a myriad of sparks before speeding away. The driver glanced back briefly, catching my gaze. He showed no signs of remorse, only hatred and determination that told me he would do it again.

I hurried from the open bay area to the break room where I punched the clock and met with the foreman for a briefing. I mentioned the Hyster incident but the foreman was convinced that it couldn't have been intentional.

The briefing was short, I knew my job well, and returning to it was like backsliding into old habits. The job had expanded during my absence, increasing my responsibilities. In addition to my former duties I was now responsible for running the splitter, as well as unclogging the main wood chipper for the mill. The added jobs meant less time on the greenchain, which was nice, and more time running the splitter, which was more like play than work.

From the C.B. radio in the splitter shack I listened to the log yard chatter while I split the cull logs from a hand operated control board. The loader operators, chop saw, and barker operators each had a C.B. which was intended for work, but used most frequently for gossip. The loader operators spoke openly, as if they didn't know I was listening, vowing to drop a log on me if they caught me off the splitter deck.

The chop saw operator chuckled over the possibility of stopping the conveyor under the chop-saw long enough to plug the chute beneath it with a mountain of log ends, and drop a log end on me when I tried to unclog it. Such attempts became routine, sometimes four to five times daily, but I was able to stand back far enough while dragging the log ends out with a pole-hook to keep from being crushed by falling log ends. The worst they could do was shower me with sawdust from the chop saw, giving me a dipped-in-batter look. The batter look seemed to amuse them, so I made a habit of dusting myself off before emerging from under the chop saw. The worst part was the sawdust that gathered in my underwear. So I stopped wearing underwear; problem solved!

*

Shellie's eyes enlarged, she sat upright in her chair. "So you don't wear underwear?"

"Well, no as a matter of fact, but I only shared because I thought I was boring you, and I assumed you weren't listening."

"And what if you have a rip in your pants?"

"I'd hate to embarrass anyone," I tried to look concerned, even sympathetic," but do you know how much you can save on apparel omitting underwear?"

An elderly woman at a table to my right had stopped chewing and was glaring at me. I cast her a casual smile, raising and lowering my eyebrows.

She abruptly turned away.

"Stop that, you're embarrassing me!" Shellie whispered as she tried to withhold a smile resulting in a look that took me pleasantly back in time.

Leaning forward she grabbed my forearm. Her eyes had widened into a more serious expression, her cheeks reddened. "By the way, 'omitting' can't be the right word for not wearing underwear!"

"Underwear," I began with faked assertiveness, "can be omitted, permitted, committed, remitted, and re-knitted, but if you emit them you might have a problem."

The elderly lady to my right, whom I had mentally dubbed Mrs. Kravits, was glaring again. I offered her an unmistakably forced smile, from which she immediately looked away.

Shellie gasped. "I can't believe you said that!"

"Admit it—admit it!" I insisted sharply, enjoying her state of helpless shock until I could contain myself no longer, and then I broke into laughter.

"Get back to your story," she demanded, shaking her head and blinking her eyes as if she were trapped in a mental quagmire between swamps of disgust and bogs of amusement.

*

Attempts on my life at the Woodville Plant were routine, and avoiding the common daily traps became routine as well. I learned to watch out for the Hyster driver, and to exercise caution under the chopsaw. Close calls became rare, although there were two attempts from which I narrowly escaped.

I was on the ground below the splitter deck when one of the loader operators sped around the corner heading straight toward me with a large log in his clamps. I spotted him only moments before he released the log, and I dove head first through the framework beneath the splitter deck. The log struck the framework with a crash that left the men on the greenchain a hundred yards away, reeling from the vibration and wondering what had happened.

Sam Welch

A few days later the main chipper for the mill became clogged, and stopped. The chipper was comprised of a huge steel wheel which turned somewhere between two-hundred and three-hundred revolutions per minute with blades capable of gnawing a large log into chips in mere seconds.

After locking out the breaker at the electrical panel, and ensuring that the chipper was secure I put on the safety harness. With an electrical hand controller I lowered myself, riding the tongs, which hung on a cable from an overhead winch, into the throat of the chipper. The chipper throat was a steel passageway through which veneer and log slabs dropped from the conveyor like water over a falls into the chipper. From there the chips went to a shaker which separated the sawdust, and then on to the mountainous chip pile, where they were pushed by a Caterpillar Tractor onto a conveyor which loaded them into trucks.

A large obstruction comprised of veneer and log slabs from the lathe had stalled the chipper. I braced myself against the chipper wheel while I hooked onto the pile of slab and veneer with the tongs and lifted it with the winch up through the chipper throat. The obstruction had barely cleared the throat when the chipper wheel started without warning. My first thought was, *this is impossible, the breaker is off, and locked out*, but there was no time for reasoning, I had to move fast. I dropped the hand controller and grasped the safety rope that held my harness.

With all the speed and strength I could muster I pulled myself, hand over hand, up the chipper throat. Suddenly the rope above me went slack and I found myself sliding back toward the chipper. Desperate to break my fall, I threw my hands and legs out catching the walls of the throat as the severed end of the safety rope fell in striking me in the face.

The chipper was almost up to speed, and I had only seconds to climb out before the conveyer would start automatically, carrying a waterfall of wood that would certainly sweep me into the chipper. I moved one hand, one leg at a time, summoning strength I didn't know I had, inching upward until I was able to grasp the top of the conveyor wall with my hand.

The conveyor started, carrying with it piles of veneer. The first pile of falling veneer scraped against me before falling into the chipper with a deafening rattle, like a Jakebrake on a Mack Truck. A cloud of dust and steam engulfed me, and stinging shards of debris pelted my legs and back.

I pulled myself past the pile of veneer and slabs which hung in the tongs, and threw my leg up and over the conveyor wall. I noticed a coworker running from the scene, and although I could only see his back as he disappeared through the grinding room door, I knew who it was and I was certain he hadn't acted alone.

I pressed the whistle button, calling for the foreman, and when he arrived I told him what had happened. We found my lock and tag laying on the ground below the electrical control panel. The lock had been cut with bolt cutters.

"It sounds like you think that someone tried to kill you, should I call the police?"

"There's the lock!" I pointed, shocked at his inability to see the obvious. "It's been cut, so what do you mean 'it sounds like I think someone tried to kill me?' I barely got out of the chipper with my skin!"

"I'm just trying to sort this all out," he growled, seeming annoyed with my impatience.

I pointed out the severed rope on the harness which appeared to have been cut with a knife, but he cast it only a passing glance, as he pulled the controller cord from the chipper throat and found only bare wires where the controller had been. "What happened to the controller?" he demanded.

I drew a fake gasp and in my best dumb redneck voice replied, "I haven't the foggiest clue. No wait!" I raised a forefinger as if a light had dawned. "I'll bet it went through the chipper!"

"This is not a joke, Welch! Now we have to get a new controller!"

Sam Welch

I was still reeling from his remark when he re-iterated, "do you want me to call the police or not?"

"Let's see if the lathe operator saw anything on his monitor, otherwise there's no witnesses, only eighty-three men who would like to see me dead!"

I followed the foreman to the lathe shack, and just as I suspected, the lathe operator hadn't seen a thing. There was no sense in calling the police, they were only impressed with successful murder attempts, and the men would only turn it against me. The best thing to do was to ride it out like a kayak on an incoming ocean wave, maintain the proper angle under the crest, savor the salt spray and the adrenaline rush, and walk away with an unbelievable story that would leave grandchildren shaking their heads and wondering how the old coot came up with such shit!

Chapter Seventeen

As the months passed I learned to expect and accept harassment, to take insults with a grain of salt, and still do my job. My enemies remained relentless, but their efforts had less effect on me.

I filled my weekends and holidays with diving, spearfishing and ocean kayaking. Ironically, I found a friend in a co-worker, George, who became my dive partner. I avoided speaking to George at the mill to keep from causing him trouble, but eventually the Union found out about our friendship and he was called forward during a Union meeting and commanded to explain why he was associating with me.

"Nobody likes you George!" someone shouted from the crowd, to which he replied, "I don't care how many of you nobodies don't like me, and just so you know, no one tells me who I can or cannot talk to!"

Amid scorns and hateful jeers George walked out of the meeting, and later resigned from the Union.

*

"Is your friend, George waiting on you now?" Shellie asked with a mild look of concern."

"I've got all the time in the world to dive," I assured her, "right now this is where I need to be. Besides, if I'm not there he dives without me and visa versa."

"Isn't that dangerous?"

"I don't think so, it's usually murky off the Oregon coast, and even if you have a partner he'll chase one fish, you'll go after another, and you'll lose sight of each other, so you might as well be alone. What's really dangerous is being with someone that you might have to rescue."

"Okay!" she said with an air that told me she didn't agree with my opinion on diving alone, and wanted to change the subject, "so tell me more about the mill, were you able to make any more friends?"

"Well yes, through a strange turn of events, his name was Scott, he was one of the loader operators, and I had to fight him before he became my friend!"

"What?" Her eyes enlarged as she leaned forward to listen.

*

The mill superintendent, 'the little shit,' had been a coach in several different sports, and most of the men that he hired were athletes of one sort or another. Some of them had played for him on various teams.

Scott, who ran the big Komatsu loader was very athletic. He was a stocky fellow who trained in mixed martial arts and boasted a dead lift of over six-hundred pounds.

One night the foreman sent me to the greenchain to fill in for a puller who had called in sick. After two hours I returned to my regular job to find the conveyor under the chop saw filled with log ends from dry buckskin logs which the chop saw operator had cut into firewood rounds for one of the guys.

Someone had stopped the conveyor to prevent the firewood from going through the lilly pad chipper. I thought I would probably end up staying late to clean up the mess.

I rolled the firewood rounds, some of them four foot in diameter, down a side chute into a loading area. Afterward I cleared the mountainous clog under the chop saw, throwing most of the regular log ends down the side chute as well since the lilly pad chipper was slow and could only chip two or three rounds at a time.

I used the 950 Caterpillar loader equipped with a large bucket to scoop up the log ends and dump them on the lilly pad pile. The process set me back hours, and afterward I was so angry that I dug a huge hole in the lilly pad pile with the loader and buried the firewood.

I was back on the 950 loader a couple of hours later when Scott drove the large Komatsu loader, forks first, into a nearby log deck. He clamped a load of logs, backed up and tossed them like pick up sticks around the log yard. I watched dumbfounded, not realizing that it was his firewood I had buried in the lilly pad pile, or that throwing logs about was a loader operator's way of having a tantrum. After clamping a second load of logs and throwing them as well, Scott parked the Komatsu, opened the cabin door, and began shouting and shaking his fist at me.

I shut off the Cat motor, opened the cabin door and listened to what he had to say.

"I'm going to come up there and throw your ass down!" Scott shouted. He sprang from the Komatsu cabin, eight feet off the ground. Landing with cat-like agility he began stomping toward me swinging his arms in a make no mistake-I mean what I say fashion. I had no reason to doubt his sincerity considering the numerous attempts on my life which I had already survived.

More than a little afraid of getting thrown off the Cat, I stepped from the cabin and jumped to the ground, landing with slightly less finesse than I intended, but after forcing a quick recovery I regained my composure, and walked steadily to meet Scott, preparing myself mentally with every step for the fight of my life.

"You fucking son of a bitch, you buried my wood in the lilly pad pile and I'm going to beat the shit out-a-you!" he shouted with clenched fists.

I stopped just out of striking range, knowing that I needed to land the first punch in order to win. "You mean over there." I pointed, feigning naivety, and at the same moment realizing that I had pointed with the wrong hand, my right, meaning that I had only my left to strike with.

He looked toward the lilly pad pile. That was my cue. I swung and missed, grazing his cheek slightly. The fight was on, and I could only hope that my sense for ducking and dodging was keener than my sucker punch.

Scott retaliated with a right cross that narrowly missed my jaw, followed by a face-level left kick which I dodged. He advanced forward with a left cross and a right kick, missing again, every punch and kick telegraphed with recoils, grunts and groans. His fighting style had an obvious pattern and rhythm. I rushed in like a child rushes into a jump rope, landing a flurry of rabbit punches on his face.

Almost immediately Scott tied me up, throwing his arms over my shoulders and trapping my arms. I wrenched and turned 180 degrees facing away from him.

Throwing the back of my head into his face, I butted *him* with all my strength. I grabbed for his fingers in order to bend them while bridging with my back to break his hold. I felt him spit on the back of my head and I knew the head butt had connected.

He tripped me and threw me to the ground. I rolled with all the liveliness I could muster out of kicking range, and sprang to my feet fists clenched and ready to fight. In my mind I had this, he was mine!

He advanced throwing the same predictable sequence of punches and kicks, right arm, left leg, left arm, right leg.

I rushed in delivering another flurry of rabbit punches to his face. Again he tied me up, and once again I turned and bridged, throwing my head. This time his face was out of range. *Quick study!* I thought as I felt myself being tripped and thrown to the ground.

Again I rolled and sprang to my feet, anxiously waiting for that opening between Scott's kicks and punches. Finding it, I rushed in a third time, punching as hard as I could at close range before his powerful arms encircled and trapped me. In a response that was becoming routine I turned and bridged. My hands quickly found his hand-lock and pried two of his fingers free. I was about to break his fingers when he shouted, seemingly out of breath, "Wait, wait let's talk."

"Talk?" I didn't want to release his fingers, *talk? Just when I had him where I wanted him?* "I'll let go if you let go," I told him.

"Okay," he agreed, relaxing his hold.

I released his fingers and turned to face him.

"You buried my firewood over there in the pile." He pointed.

As I glanced at the pile, a solid right cross struck me in the jaw, staggering me sideways. I recovered quickly, and skipped toward him as he backed away, holding his hands in a pleading fashion, while shouting, "Wait, wait!"

"Wait for what, for you to hit me?" I shouted back.

"I'm not going to hit you again, but you had that one coming! You buried my firewood in the pile, and then you hit me with a sucker punch, so now we're even!" He extended his hand, "Let's shake and call it good."

"Let's not!" I suggested as I stepped back, holding my hands palms out rejecting his handshake. "And if you so much as clench a fist I'll be back on you like stink on shit."

"Fair enough!" He nodded, adding, "You were wrong to bury my firewood."

I spat angrily, and stepped forward, re-clenching my fists. "By cutting that firewood and stopping that conveyor while I was working on the greenchain, you set me back hours. I'll probably have to work late to make up for it. If you want to cut firewood then throw it out yourself, and don't make my job harder!"

He drew a deep breath and released a sigh. "I didn't know you were on the greenchain. I'm sorry. I'll throw out my own wood from now on." Again he offered his hand.

I shook briefly, released it and walked away, still feeling like I wanted to finish that fight.

Later that night I heard millworkers boasting and laughing that Scott had kicked my ass.

Sam Welch

After punching the time clock I found him alone and called him out, "If you're going to spread rumors about how you kicked my ass then let's make it official! We'll see who gets their ass kicked!"

His expression seemed sincere, perhaps humble. "I never said anything like that, I never thought it, and that's not how I feel. I have a pretty good idea who might be spreading those rumors, and I promise you I'll set him straight."

"Good enough," I said with a nod, realizing that Scott had offered me greater veneration than I could expect from anyone else in the mill.

*

Shellie shook her head and rolled her eyes in that all-knowing manner that made me realize that she saw me as just one more male ego on a pride trip.

"What!" I countered, displaying my best dumbfounded expression.

"Well?" She paused as if she were waiting for me to explain myself, but before I could squeeze out a word she added, "was there ever a time when the bait was there and you didn't bite?"

I could see that she lacked understanding of the "challenge" from the male standpoint. Such things cannot easily be explained to a woman, but I decided to try; "If you back down once, then every asshole who thinks he's tough will want a piece of you. Believe me, I used to ascribe to, 'It takes a bigger man to walk away from a fight.' Trust me it's a fallacy!"

"Okay," she shook her head, "Tell me about the time you didn't take the bait."

"I'd rather tell you about the time I avoided a fight by standing my ground!"

She shook her head and peered at me through all knowing eyes, and I knew I had her attention.

*

Scott was sharing something he'd read in a tabloid over the C.B. radio, "They think they've found Jesus' body," he said.

126

J. D., the barker operator, a large powerful man, commented, "I'd like to read that tabloid."

The topic went deeply against the grain of my inner being, and although I seldom used the C.B., I grabbed the Microphone and responded, "They haven't found Jesus' body! Jesus rose body and spirit and he is physically seated at the right hand of the Father in heaven!" "I don't know if I can believe that," said Scott.

"If you can't believe it, then you can't have salvation!" I snapped.

J. D. cut in, "I have half a notion to go over to the splitter shack and kick that little fucker's ass, but he'd probably run like a chicken shit."

I felt myself bristle as I picked up the mic. "Come on over and kick my ass J. D., I promise not to run!"

"Kicking Welch's ass isn't as easy as you think J. D.," Scott warned.

I stepped outside the shack, onto the catwalk and waited, but J. D., who probably could have beat me effortlessly, was a no show.

*

"I guess boys will be boys no matter what," said Shellie.

"I guess so," I replied, keeping my expression as matter-of-fact as I could make it.

"So what happened to 'turn the other cheek?' I guess what I'm saying is,
I can't understand the male ego, and the pride thing."

I felt a tinge of regret. "Well, you are right, and in fact the Lord gave me an earth shaking warning."

"A what?"

I nodded a confirmation. "I dreamt one night that I was praying with my mother when I heard a voice booming down from overhead. The voice was very audible and literally shook everything. It shook me upright, and wide awake in my bed. The voice said, 'You're too proud!' I didn't understand it at the time, and I don't completely understand it now, but I acknowledge before you and God that you are right. I definitely have a pride problem which goes much deeper than just male ego, and I am working on it. As for J. D. and turning the other cheek, I probably would have dodged a couple of his punches before I smacked him back."

"That's interesting." She seemed to ponder my words for a moment with a look that was neither accepting nor condemning, and then repeated, "boys will be boys!"

Chapter Eighteen

The safety committee was a joke in the eyes of the men. Elected members attended regular meetings where much was said, but little was done.

When the time rolled around to elect the members, a meeting of all the workers was held in the mechanic's shop. I was nominated and elected by unpopular vote amid scornful laughter and ridicule.

During my first safety meeting, the foreman asked me if I had any safety concerns for the mill.

"Yes," I said as I addressed the four other elected members, the Foreman, and the Head Millwright, "the dryer sprinkler system uses all the available water to extinguish fires inside the dryer, and the fire system takes eight minutes to reset before there is enough pressure to run a fire hose. If a dryer fire spreads into the truss above the dryer it could accelerate out of control before the system could be reset, and there won't be enough water to put it out!"

"You don't know what the fuck you're talking about!" the Head Millwright cut in, shouting and shaking his index finger at me.

"I think I do know what I'm talking about!" I countered, almost as loud.

"Okay, okay," the Foreman leaned forward in his seat motioning for calm by waving his arm between us. "So what do you propose we do to remedy this situation, Sam?"

"I propose we keep a small tanker truck close by and ready in case of emergency."

"You idiot," the Millwright cut in, "the fire department is right down the road, they can be here in thirty seconds!"

Some of the other committee members shook their heads in a clear gesture that told me they agreed with the Head Millwright.

After the meeting one of the committee members approached me and said, "I told them the same thing two weeks ago, but they wouldn't listen." He turned quickly and walked away to keep from being seen talking to me.

*

Shellie drew a deep breath and sat upright. "I think I know what this is leading to. Were you working at that mill that burned down in Woodville?"

"Yes." I nodded with some disappointment. The kind of disappointment a comedian feels when someone in the audience blurts out his punchline and ruins the joke.

*

I was in my yard when I noticed the plume of smoke that darkened a portion of the sky. I hopped in my old truck and hurried down toward the mill. The fire department had blocked off a large area including the main roadway, but I watched from the roadside at a distance as the complex turned to embers within a couple of hours.

The dryer off-bearer, still wearing his apron and gloves, walked over and stood beside me. With shaking hands he drew a cigarette from a half crushed package. "You don't suppose anyone would mind if I smoke do you?"

"I don't suppose so," I said, adding, "You're still wearing your apron and gloves."

"I'm still on the clock," he said as he lit his cigarette.

"How did it start?"

"It started in the dryer and after we flooded the dryer it spread to the truss. We couldn't reset the system fast enough to get any pressure, and by the time we did it was too late."

I shook my head. *My words had been wasted and traded for ridicule. I-told-you-sos would be useless and moot.* "I should have brought marshmallows!" I said."

"Sounds good right about now," said the dryer tender, "I lost my lunch-pail in there."

*

Shellie nestled in her chair. "What did you do for work after the mill burned down?"

"They moved some of us including myself to the big plant in Medford, where I worked graveyard shift on one of the dryers for six months. The work was good for a while since few people knew me as a scab. But when the Union contract expired, and the proverbial lines were drawn in the sand, despite my low profile, I became popular once again. Threats, and even attempts to harm me were made by people I didn't even know. When negotiations failed the men and women, perhaps four hundred in all, voted to strike. Yours truly, in a fit of defiance decided to be the first person to cross that picket line."

"Really?" Shellie straightened.

"Really!" I confirmed with a nod.

"Isn't that wrong, to cross a picket line, I mean?"

"Try looking at the Rottweiler from the fire hydrant's perspective instead of the other way around!"

"What?" She grimaced and shook her head. "I hardly think that a prism of light through a yellow splatter on the backdrop of a dog's inner thigh is a good metaphor for crossing a picket line."

"Okay!" I chuckled and nodded, realizing that the years had left her wit and intellect intact. "If I have a job," I said, "and I'm expected to show up on time, who has the right, besides my employer to threaten me and tell me I can't work? Couple all of that with the abuse I put up with, and what would you expect me to do?"

"Well, knowing you—you'd cross that picket line!" she said.

Sam Welch

*

It was 10:45 PM on the 26th of July 1993, and the cool summer breeze that found its way through my truck window served to numb me to the task that lay before me.

As I approached the plywood plant with its open cyclone gate I surveyed the crowd of three hundred picketers blocking the road. Some carried signs, others baseball bats, cans of spray paint, and gunny sacks containing ten pounds of ice. The idea behind the gunny sack filled with ice is that if they beat someone to death with a bag of ice the evidence melts away.

Across the street, parked in a row, were three Medford City Police cars, and at least as many police, all facing the fray.

I kept my window down to show the mob I wasn't afraid. When the traffic light turned green I turned from the highway and came to a stop at the edge of the picket line.

A hush fell over the crowd which stood in front of me and on both sides of my truck. Every face mirrored the same astonished expression, shock that anyone would dare to cross their picket line.

I broke the silence, nodding at a couple of the guys, "Dave, Joe, nice night eh?"

"Where do you think you're going?" one man asked.

"Goin' to work!" I chuckled.

"There ain't no work tonight, so you might as well turn around and go home!"

"Nope, I'm goin' to work," I assured him, adding a nod for all to see.

"So, you think you're goin' to cross our picket line?" said another.

"Yep! That is exactly what I'm doin'."

There was another moment of silence, a brief calm—shattered by the high pitched, trailer park voice of a woman shouting, "What's wrong with all of ya'! He ain't nuthin' but a fuckin' scab, get him!"

The crowd came to life stumbling over one another to get to my truck. Several men climbed onto the hood, hammering with whatever they had,

132

and spray painting the windows. A group of men climbed in the bed and began beating on the roof. Someone yelled, "tip him over!" The truck began to rock violently, as they counted, "one, two three, lift," but the crowd on the opposite side was trying to tip it the other direction, and the two groups counteracted one another causing the truck to bounce like a basketball with every heave.

I kept the truck in gear at little more than an idle, and each time the wheels touched the ground the truck moved forward slightly.

Aside from a few loogies that found their way thru the window I remained unharmed. The mob with all their fury could do no more than beat the hell out of my truck. Within a few moments I had passed through the gate where the crowd could not follow.

After jumping from my pickup bed, the strikers armed themselves with rocks and waited for me to get out of the truck.

Pulling into the parking lot I noticed several other cars scattered about and I realized I wasn't the first to cross the picket line. Dozens of rocks landed around me as I stepped out of the truck, some were 5 to 6 inches thick.

I hurried into the safety of the building as rocks struck the wall behind me with loud thuds.

Waiting inside the door were five other mill workers. One of them, a sturdy man with prematurely greying hair patted my shoulder and said, "I don't see how you and those balls of yours could possibly have fit in that little truck!"

No one laughed except me, and as I surveyed the faces of the five men, I noticed three of them were visibly quivering. "What a rush," I said, "I have half a notion to go back and do it again!"

"You could have got yourself killed!" one of the men blurted, noticeably annoyed at my statement.

"Staring down a threat with blatant in-your-face defiance is hard to kill!" I snapped, "But you guys crossed the picket line too, didn't you?"

They all shook their heads, and Jake, the guy who patted my shoulder responded with, "No, we're on the spreader crew. We were working late when the strike began, so we were caught behind the picket line and didn't want to cross back through the mob to leave here."

I took Jake for the leader of the group. He had the looks and the calm assurance in his voice that people look up to and follow.

"You're all going to continue working through this strike aren't you? I mean you're not going to back down now that you have that 'scab' label, are you?" Halfway through the question I wished I could rephrase it to sound less desperate but it was too late, so I decided to continue and make a total ass of myself, "I mean it might as well be tattooed on your foreheads now.
You're all scabs just like me."

The simple truth was, I needed them!

Jake motioned to one of the men, "Brad here is not so sure. He thinks he'd rather strike than cross the picket line. The rest of us will probably carpool in some old junk car so they can't ruin anything of value. The bottom line is, we can't afford to strike, we got bills to pay, and within a few weeks most of those strikers are going to realize they need the work too!"

Jake's words comforted me in a strange way. We were not totally helpless, we had a plan.

The five of them showed me how to lay up veneer, how the components of plywood are stacked cross-wise, glued, pressed and cut into four by eight plywood sheets.

We worked together and I, an amateur working with professionals, did my best to keep up. The six of us bonded like soldiers behind enemy lines, brothers facing the same foe.

When break time rolled around we went together to the break room where the vending machines offered a wide assortment of goodies and refreshments.

I was seated at one of the tables when I heard someone, with a wrestlemaniac voice shouting my name from outside the steel meshed window.

A smarter man would have ignored it, but in a foolish moment I wandered over to the window.

"Sam Welch!" a hulking body builder of a man growled from the sidewalk ten feet away. He wore a tank top which clung tight over massive pectoralis muscles and six pack abs. His rippled arms glistened with a baby oil glow in the light of the street lamps. "We're going to kill you! We're going to kill your wife and kids! We're going to burn down your house!
We're going to kill your dogs and your cat!"

With one hand I grabbed the steel mesh and pulled myself close to the window while pointing at him with the index finger on my free hand. "I AM going to kill you!" I blurted matter-of-factly, and if not for the grated window I probably would have.

A puzzled look fell over his face, his jaw dropped in shock.

"The next time I see you, whether on the street, or in your gymnasium, or in your bed at night. I won't rest till I find you, and you won't get away from me!" I shouted.

In the brief moment before my five co-workers dragged me away from the window I savored the look of shock and fear on that man's face.

The co-workers pulled me outside the break room and held me down on the concrete floor until they were certain that I had calmed down before they released me.

"Who was that guy!" I asked as I struggled to get to my feet.

"Never seen him before. He must be a union goon," said Jake, "They find these guys in the local gymnasiums and hire them to threaten scabs.

"Lucky thing there's a steel grate over that window," I muttered, confident I could have taken him.

"lucky for you!" one of the men said with a chuckle.

"No, lucky for him," I countered.

"Chances are he didn't mean a word he said," Jake responded.

"Of course not," I replied, "I don't have a cat!"

Later in the shift the company vice president paid us a visit. He was tall, early middle aged and well groomed. We shut down the presses and sat on stacks of plywood while he spoke.

"It's dangerous crossing the picket line at night!" he began, as if we didn't already know.

I almost blurted, "No shit!" but I bit my lip to hold it in.

He continued with, "We have another offer to set on the table with the Union. It's a good offer, and if they don't accept it we'll move everyone that crosses the line to day shift starting Monday morning."

I didn't want to interrupt, but his light blue shirt and slacks remained unwrinkled and every hair on his head seemed well placed. I raised my hand and without waiting for him to call on me, forced, "How the hell did you get in here?"

He laughed. "There's a back gate from the white house (the main office), I snuck in. You guys are welcome to use that gate as well.

"Not me. I'm crossin' that picket line," I said, "and I don't care if nobody else does!"

"That's probably the best way," he agreed, adding, "just make sure you don't speed or run over anybody because the cops are watching and waiting for you to step out of line. I strongly suggest that you carpool."

"Anyone who wants to ride with me is welcome," I offered, although no one took me up on it.

The V. P. answered a few more questions and afterward spoke with Jake about having enough materials, glue and veneer to keep our small crew running. He promised to provide everything we needed, and to have the traffic light at the picket line turn green at an appointed time to keep us from being stopped in the picket line at a red light, and then he left.

We worked through the night, talking and joking as if we had all known one another for years. The hours passed like minutes until the morning light signaled the end of the shift.

We lined our vehicles bumper to bumper and crossed in a row to prevent strikers from getting between us. Jake sped across first in his black Beamer. One striker hurried from his path to keep from being run over. A horn blast and rude gestures were exchanged. I followed a close second with the other cars following in turn, smiling and waving at everyone with a half rotation hand wave, the kind of wave festival princesses do in a parade. My friendliness went unappreciated.

The strikers were fewer in number than the night before, and crossing was easier, almost uneventful in comparison.

The rest of the week yielded more of the same—the same brutal picket line, the same death threats, the same small group of men sharing a deeper bond of friendship, laughter, and stories of defiance.

Dayshift on Monday presented a change in tactics—a new game on a new playing field.

As I pulled out of my driveway early Monday morning, I realized I was being followed. Shortly after getting on the freeway several vehicles overtook me. I didn't recognize any of the drivers, but the car in front slowed me to a crawl while the jacked up 4x4 to my left attempted to run me off the road.

The tailgater in the rear turned his high beam on me while laying on his horn. What they didn't realize was that I didn't care if my truck got damaged, and that I was more adept at this game than they were. I simply slammed on my brakes and watched the tailgater in my rear view mirror careening off the road as I parnellied around the big 4x4.

At each on ramp more vehicles joined in the effort to overtake and trap me, and what began with a few cars became a huge game of chicken from which I emerged victorious, successfully crossing the picket line unharmed.

I spoke with the company vice president about the incident, and he promised to alert the State Police.

Goons continued following me on the freeway for several days, although their attempts to harm me became less frequent.

Sam Welch

Dayshift lessened the danger in crossing the picket line proving to me that evil people won't do in the daylight the things they'll do at night.

During the second week more workers abandoned their pickets and crossed the line. This took the spotlight off of me, while causing them more ridicule and shame from their union cronies. One scab after another approached me and apologized, often adding that they had always respected me for the stand I had taken. I found very little sympathy for these wishy-washy turncoats willing to kill me one minute and hug me the next.

My friend Scott, the loader operator, also crossed the picket line. According to his widow he was receiving threats when he died in a motorcycle accident. He apparently went off a rural roadway and crashed. There were no witnesses.

By the third week of the strike more than ninety men and women had crossed the picket line and the workers were called to assemble in the mill conference room. We were provided with a synopsis, pencil and clipboard for an indoctrination by a detective on the city police force. It turned out that one of the scabs had been arrested and was facing charges, possibly even prison time for communicating a threat. He had placed his hand on a gun which was laying on his dash while his car was being bashed on the picket line.

After being introduced by the company vice president the detective introduced himself again, and began to advise us of our rights as scabs, and what we could and could not do. The rest of the crowd seemed content to listen quietly as he spoke, but a deep anger welled up within me, and when I could stand the bullshit no longer I raised my hand. He saw me, but neglected to call on me so I stood to my feet with my hand raised and interrupted, "excuse me!"

"You have a question?" he asked.

"Yes I do! You haven't told us what our rights are, you've told us what our rights aren't!"

I was more than a little shocked to hear the crowd behind me voice their loud approval, and I waited for their shouts and applause to simmer before I continued, "Your men sit across from that picket line daily and do nothing as our cars are vandalized and our lives are threatened." Again I had to wait for the shouting and applause to die.

"Now you're telling us that we don't have the right to defend ourselves!" The crowd backed me once again.

The detective pointed an angry finger at me and snapped, "You said you had a question! All you've given me are angry comments."

"I do have a question!" I retorted with equal venom, "Is your police department union?"

The audience reaffirmed my question, demanding an answer.

"I am not union!" he proclaimed. His eyes shifted from side to side surveying the group, and then he added, "because I am management, but yes, in answer to your question, our department is union!"

The crowd erupted with one voice in an angry uproar, throwing anything they could get their hands on, pens, pencils, clipboards, apples and oranges at the detective.

He tried unsuccessfully to duck and dodge the flying objects in a dancing fashion with his hands in front of his face, until the company vice president stepped forward to escort him out while shielding his head with a clipboard.

Before he reached the door several chairs flew his direction narrowly missing him.

Before the strike ended I heard a rumor from a very reliable source. One of the company owners had flown out from Texas. He was standing on the front porch of the White House (the main office building) looking at the mob on the picket line when one of the strikers threw a rock narrowly missing his head.

He walked back inside the office and said, "We're going to shut this place down and liquidate it!"

Sam Welch

Closing a business because of a strike was illegal according to federal guidelines, but the owners cited environmental concerns, market woes, and even the spotted owl controversy, and within a matter of months after the strike ended the plant closed its doors forever.

*

"That's quite a story," said Shellie. "So now you're out of work?"

"No, I've been working."

"Where did you go after the mill closed?"

"Enough about me. I want to hear about you," I told her.

A look of disappointment fell over her face. "I'll tell you my story, but first finish yours! I want to hear what you've been doing since the mill closed down."

Her reasons sounded genuine enough, although the sadness in her eyes told me there was a deeper story that she wasn't anxious to tell. I dismissed my suspicions quickly, I could ramble on about myself all day, and as long as no one objected I would. "Well, I went back to school for several months. I studied diesel mechanics, but when the spring term ended I went to work for a movie crew."

"A what?" She straightened in her chair. "It sounded like you said that you went to work for a movie crew!"

"Yup! A friend of mine at the Visitor's Convention Center hooked me up with the Location Manager. I started off clearing weeds around a large building that doubled as an office for the Art Director and Location Manager. The building had a large garage where props were stored."

"Props?"

"You know, things used on the set. The movie was about a family that gets kidnapped on the river, so the props were things like tents, rubber rafts, camping and river equipment."

"It seems to me I heard something about that movie. Is that the one starring Meryl Streep and Kevin Bacon, where she's some kind of river guide, and he's a crook?"

"Yep, that's the one." I nodded.

"Did you get to meet Meryl Streep?" Shellie didn't wait for me to answer, but continued with, "I've always loved her movies! She's such a talented actress!"

"Yep, I met her, although we were never properly introduced, but you're getting ahead of me."

"Okay, I'll shut up and listen." She nestled in her chair and leaned forward with the expression of a child hell bent on a bedtime story. Naturally I felt compelled to deliver.

Chapter Nineteen

The weeds were tall and gangly making the weed eating process slow and tedious. A continuous cloud of dust, pollen, and itchy plant fragments found a way into my clothes, but the work was repetitive and required little thought, allowing my mind time to wander and my imagination to run free. I enjoyed the hard work, it was aerobic, and by midday I felt like I'd been to the gym and was getting paid for it. How cool was that?

The office girl came and went. She was young, blond and beautiful. Her pretty face, nice shape and height reminded me of the Fraulein from Hogan's Heroes, and yet she displayed an attitude of disgust toward me that made me think perhaps I looked like her ex-husband.

She spoke to me only when she had a message from Fred, the Art Director, or in answer to a question, and even then with a tone of distaste. Clearly she was too sophisticated to share a polite smile or a kind word with a common weed cutter.

Fred, the Art Director had a friendly look about him. He was middle aged, slim, medium height and mildly balding. He had a keen intellect and bubbling sense of humor characterized by a boisterous laugh that gave him away as nothing short of genuine.

Josh, one of the two Location Managers was a younger man, thirty five-ish. He was tall and lanky, very intelligent and focused on getting the job done. Both he and Fred treated me with more respect than I was accustomed to. They liked my work, and finding the fire break that I had cut around the building adequate to satisfy the Fire Marshall, they asked me to go with them and look over six of the film sites along the Rogue River.

They seemed mindless of the poison oak strewn along the deer trails although I pointed it out to them as we made our way into the chosen areas.

The sites were overgrown with brush and cluttered with winter debris and garbage. They needed someone to clean it up and clear the excess brush.

"Do you think you could hire a few of your friends and clean up these film sites?" Fred asked.

"Of course I can," I told him.

I wasted no time assembling a small crew, and equipping them with chainsaws, weed eaters and garbage bags.

Dereck, one of the men I hired had worked with me at the mill. We weren't exactly friends, but Dereck asked me for a job, and I knew him to be a good worker so I hired him.

The operation took the better part of three weeks and a lot of hard work, but Fred and Josh were very pleased with the end result.

During the clearing process I learned that the movie was a high budget film with an all-star cast.

The cast and crew were away filming along a river in Montana. They were scheduled to move back to Southern Oregon in July to complete the film along the Rogue River. Fred and Josh had been left behind to prepare for the return of the cast and crew.

It was only the third week of May, but the Southern Oregon grass was already drying and turning brown, while the grass and scenery along the river in Montana was green. They needed the scenery to match. This created a dilemma that left Fred and Josh scratching their heads.

Josh asked me to take a ride with him and look over the film sites to see if we could formulate a plan.

"The jet boat company is willing to blast these film sites," said Josh,

"They want $750 per day for the jet boat, and two hundred apiece for a two man crew. The problem is that the film is already ten million over budget, and it's not even halfway done."

"What do you mean by 'blast these film sites'?" I asked.

"They want us to mount a large water pump on one of their jet boats along with a fire hose to blast water over the sites. In short they think we're rich and they want too much money. Now I was thinking if you have a raft that could carry the pump and hoses then you might be able to do the job for a hundred bucks a day and save the company a lot of money. The BLM wouldn't give me permission to irrigate, but I was able to obtain a fire suppression permit, so if anybody should ask, we're not irrigating." "I have a Zodiac raft, and I'd sure like to give it a try," I said.

"Okay, give the raft a try, and let me know how it works, but once we get the ball rolling there are some rules that we have to go by. One of them is, that you're not allowed to do this alone. There has to be two men in the boat for safety purposes, so you'll have to find a second guy preferably someone with experience on the river. There's a hundred dollars a day in it for each of you."

"I know just the guy!" I said, "Dereck, who worked with me clearing the film sites, might be willing. He's been a guide on the upper Rogue. I'll give him a call."

"Sounds good, keep me posted."

As soon as I got home I dialed Dereck. He liked the idea and although he couldn't make it the following day, he agreed to the job.

The next morning I had my wife follow me as I picked up the pump and fire hose from the local armory where the production company was building a set for one of the movie scenes.

The pump was an eleven horse Briggs and Stratton, and along with 150 feet of fire hose it was very heavy. Too heavy I suspected, for the Zodiac, but I had to give it a try.

I drove to Hog Creek Boat Landing, where I launched and loaded the gear into the Zodiac at the water's edge.

After securing the Zodiac to a clump of willows I drove the truck and boat trailer down to a take-out spot just above Graves Creek. I parked the truck and rode back with Carmen to Hog Creek. After a goodbye kiss, and a wave I was off allowing the current to carry me downstream.

The first film site was at the mouth of Hellgate about a hundred yards below Hog Creek Boat Landing. I was able, after some difficulty, to maneuver the Zodiac using the oars to carry me from the fast water into the eddy that bordered the site.

After connecting the hoses, and tossing the intake hose with foot valve overboard, I fired up the noisy pump. When I opened the nozzle I had to brace myself from the impact as the hose fired a heavy jet of water high over the dry ground. The mist fell back over me like a mild rain, causing me to shiver in the morning chill. I repositioned myself upwind and continued watering. Within half an hour the entire film site was drenched, from high on the hillside to the water's edge.

I shut off the pump, loaded the fire hose and shoved off once again, backing desperately with the oars into the fast water at the top of the eddy. I fought to clear the large boulders surrounding the opening to Hellgate where the river funneled rapidly through a small passageway into a deep narrow canyon with high cliff walls that blocked the sun.

After passing through the narrow rocks at the canyon's entrance the water slowed to a leisurely flow. Several hundred yards downstream the steep cliffs gave way to a broader canyon with sloping walls.

From the South Bank Hog Creek cascaded down the mountain into a pool at the river's edge where the terrain bordered a long sandbar strewn with willows. This was one of our film sites. Grabbing the bow rope which was draped over one of the pontoons, I stepped into the water, tossed the foot valve and intake overboard, and pulled the Zodiac to the water's edge. The pump motor roared to life on the first tug and the fire hose immediately stiffened. I pulled the hose from the Zodiac, opened the nozzle and thoroughly drenched the hillside and the surrounding sandbar.

After draining and recoiling the hose in the Zodiac I shoved off and headed downstream. The river widened and moved faster over shallow rocks creating a brutal rollercoaster ride that slammed the pump up and down like a battering ram against the Zodiac's wooden floor. I began to realize that the Zodiac was not sufficient for the job. I needed a bigger boat, something that drew very little water and could pass over low lying rocks.

Jet boats loaded with tourists zipped by, skimming over the shallows with ease. Tourists waved, while the guides glared with envy, and I realized that they knew I had under bid them. Intermittent rafters and kayakers came and went voicing friendly casual greetings and comments.

The next stop was Taylor Creek where tufts of river grass grew atop rock outcrops scattered like stepping stones at the river's edge. At the lower end of the site a gravel beach tapered gradually into a steeper hillside that gave way to a grassy knoll. I watered the entire area, spraying jets of water high above the horizontal pan of any normal camera.

The fourth film site was downstream, on the north bank above Ennis Riffle, where tall trees covered a flat area creating a beautiful natural campsite. The spot could only be reached by boat, and few people knew of it.

Grass was scarce, but Josh had wanted it watered nonetheless. He also wanted a tent pitched on the site so other campers would know it was occupied and think twice before setting up camp.

The next two film sites were near Argo Riffle on the North Bank. The first was an extended flat grassy area at the base of a steep hillside. The second was just below it where two huge rock outcrops formed what seemed an uncanny border between mountain and river.

I finished watering and found my truck and trailer at the take out spot just above Graves Creek.

After loading the Zodiac and pulling it from the river I noticed the bottom had been badly damaged by the rocks. I needed a jet boat, but jet boats were spendy, and beyond the reach of an unemployed millworker.

146

That evening I called Josh. "The Zodiac won't work!" I told him.

"As much as I hate to, it looks as if I'll have to cave in to the jet boat company," he said.

I didn't know what else to tell him, but I thanked him for giving me a chance at the job, and as I hung up I felt a knot tugging at my gut. *If I had a boat—I had a job! If I didn't have a boat—I didn't have a job! I had to get a boat!*

I hit redial. The phone seemed to ring louder than usual, and I realized it was because I had it pressed tight against my ear with jittery fingers. I tried to relax as it rang again.

Josh picked up. "Hello."

"Hi Josh—give me a day to get a boat!"

"I was hoping you'd say that." He laughed.

"Thanks, bye!" I hung up the phone, and only on second thought did I realize how rude I had been, but calling back to apologize seemed equally awkward, so I left it at that.

I searched the newspapers under "buy and sell." Jet boats were over ten thousand dollars. One add caught my eye. It wasn't a jet boat, it was a drift boat, $1300. A local guide was buying a new boat and needed to sell his old one. The boat was aluminum, a guide model which meant it had a solid 5/8 inch floor instead of the standard ½ inch floor.

Drift boats were flat bottomed, they drew only a few inches of water which enabled them to glide over shallow rocks. The draw backs were that a drift boat won't bounce off rocks like a raft, and the boat, if not handled properly, could easily capsize and sink in the rapids.

I checked with the credit union, two thousand was the most I could get on a signature loan. I took it, and went to see the boat. It was perfect. I paid the man and shook his hand. He threw in an old pair of oars, they weren't the best but they were enough to get started with.

I called Dereck and told him I had a boat.

"I've changed my mind!" he said, "I've decided I don't want to work with you!"

"Why not?"

"You scabbed and took this job from my friends who run the jet boats just like you scabbed at the mill, and you don't know that eight mile stretch of river. It's a lot more treacherous than you think. You don't know how to use the sticks! You're going to capsize that boat and kill yourself, and I hope you do!" He hung up with a loud click.

Regaining my composure took a minute. I had one more option, Carmen had a friend whose husband, John was an avid fisherman. He had his own drift boat which meant that he knew something about handling the oars, or "sticks" as they were called, and John was out of work.

Carmen looked up the number, and I gave John a call.

"I'd like to give it a try," said John, "but I don't know that stretch of river."

"How hard can it be?" I asked, wondering if everyone else was a little crazy or if it was just me.

"Harder than you think, but I'll give it a try."

The following morning I took the boat to the armory where the carpenters for the movie crew were going to build a mount for the pump.

Josh was there with the head Carpenter. He glared at me in a confronting manner and pointed. "That's not a jet boat!" he blurted with a tone of shock that left me a bit insecure.

I swallowed hard as I searched my mind for the right words. I knew I was on shaky ground, merely a sentence away from being unemployed.

The Head Carpenter rescued me as he slapped the side of the boat, "Nope, she's better than a jet boat! This here is a drift boat, much like the original Mackenzie River boat only better. She'll draw less than three inches of water and slide down those rapids so smoothly that no one will know that she came or went!"

An open-mouthed look of surprise crossed Josh's face as he glanced from me to the Head Carpenter and back again.

I gave him my best *I-knew-it-all-along* nod and wink.

"We'll have her mounted and ready for you by noon today," said the Head Carpenter.

I thanked him and Josh and walked away breathing a sigh of relief, and thanking God for the opportunity.

Around one P.M. I met John at the boat landing. After launching we tied the boat to willows at the water's edge. John followed me in his car as I drove my pickup and trailer to the take out spot below Argo Riffle. When we returned in John's car to the boat landing I noticed John was more than a bit nervous while I was filled with a Tom Sawyer/Huck Finn's maiden voyage kind of excitement.

When John was seated at the oars I shoved off and jumped over the bow into the boat.

The swift water carried us rapidly toward the first film site at the mouth of Hellgate. John narrowly made the eddy in time to keep us from being swept through the funnel-like opening at Hellgate's mouth, but once inside the eddy we went from fast water stress to a calm that matched the slow swirling eddy.

As John brought the boat to shore I tossed the foot valve over one side and hurled the firehose over the other. Taking the bow rope, I jumped out and tied the boat to a clump of willows, and then I straightened the hose and made sure the nozzle was closed.

I tossed a few congratulatory words John's way as I fired up the pump. The hose stiffened and straightened. When I opened the nozzle the pump motor rose from an idle to a roar as it forced a massive stream of water seventy feet beyond the nozzle.

Within twenty minutes the film site had been drenched several times over and we were ready to load up and cast off.

John took his place at the oars and we shoved off again.

The fast water caught us at the edge of the eddy and carried us through the mouth of Hellgate. We scraped against the side of the rock but sustained little damage.

149

Sam Welch

At the base of Hellgate we watered the Hog Creek film site and started downstream through Dunn Riffle, the first real rapids that we had encountered.

The boat began to bounce like a roller coaster, and halfway through the riffle we struck a rock and turned sideways. The chine wedged against another rock sending the bow upward, throwing me into a summersault that carried me past John all the way to the stern. The force of the water turned us on edge at a forty-five degree angle. I regained my footing and grabbed an oar in an attempt to pry us free from the rock, while John stood upright on the inner chine, clinging to the upside of the boat, a look of fear and uncertainty on his face.

We had taken on a large quantity of water when a twenty five foot jet boat zipped past us creating a wake that did little to help our situation. I heard laugher and cheering over the roar of fast water, and I recognized Dereck along with four jet boat employees in the jet boat. They turned around below the rapids and headed back up river, shouting and spraying us with water as they whipped past us.

My prying with the oar was not enough to free us from the rock, and I knew that one more pass with the jet boat could capsize us.

I shouted at John, "Climb up and put your weight on the bow."

"I'm not getting up there," John replied, a look of terror in his eyes.

"Get up there before I beat you to death with this fucking oar!"

John complied and climbed onto the bow. His weight and my prying helped to free the boat from the rock, and she slipped back upright, but remained badly foundered. I grabbed a five gallon bucket and bailed with all my strength as the rapids carried us downstream crashing us into one rock after another.

Again the jet boat sped past us, the crew mocking and shouting. Their wake brought water over the side of the boat, sinking us completely, but the force of the rapids worked in our favor, carrying the boat over shallow rocks, bringing the sides above water long enough for me to bail the excess and bring us back afloat.

I must have bailed several hundred gallons before we were able to drift ashore on a sandbar at the bottom of the rapids.

The jet boaters made one last pass, yelling scornful insults while John and I sat drenched and exhausted on the sandbar.

"If they come by again I'm going to fire up the pump and blast 'em good!" I said.

John rose to his feet. "Well you'll do it without me, because I quit!"

"Please don't quit John. I'm sorry that I threatened to beat you to death with the oar. I was only joking."

John gasp and glared at me with a look that wreaked of astonishment. He shook his head and said, "It's not just that, it's that you're crazy, you're fucking crazy! You're going to kill yourself, but I'm not going to die with you!"

He threw his drenched jacket over his shoulder as he turned and started to walk away. Stopping briefly he looked back and in a much calmer voice said, "I'll hike back up to the road from here and walk back to my car."
I sat for a moment after John left collecting my thoughts and wondering how I should proceed. I couldn't quit I had too much to lose. I remained convinced that rowing a boat down river could not be that difficult, you simply enter the "V" in the riffle, avoid the rocks, and keep the bow pointed downstream.

The afternoon sun warmed me and helped to lighten my clothes. When I had reached a mental crossroad between the fear of not getting done before dark or succumbing to my jitters, I arose from the safety of the warm sand and used the pump to empty my half swamped boat.

With a shove I pushed away from shore and hurled myself over the bow. I was not a natural, but I had half a mile before the next rapids to become one-with-the-sticks.

I rowed successfully from film site to film site, struggling with stress as I passed through each rapid, only to recover when the water slowed.

Every conquered riffle represented a mental milestone, an added feather in my cap of self-confidence. I blasted film site after film site, encountering few obstacles until I reached Argo riffle, where I struck a rock and knocked a small hole in the bow.

I surveyed the damage as I pulled the boat from the water at my take out spot. The hole was small enough that I could patch it with Marinetex and keep on working.

The following Morning I launched early and tied the boat to a clump of willows that bordered the Hog Creek launch ramp. I had Carmen follow me and bring me back from the take out spot where I left my truck and trailer. The work went smoothly, although it took me ten hours to complete the job. Again I struck a rock at Argo riffle, denting the boat chine but I allowed myself to think of it as collateral damage, and lost no sleep because it.

Over the course of the next two weeks I realized that I could take out at Ennis Riffle and launch again at Almeda Park, cutting off four miles of river and still water all the film sites. Carmen wasn't happy about returning after five hours to juggle vehicles, but she helped me nonetheless.

I involved Josh as little as possible, telling him only that the watering was being completed daily as planned, but when the jet boat guys told him about my incident at Dunn Riffle he called to check up on me.

He began with, "Fred and I visited the film sites the other day. We could see they're well watered, and new grass is already beginning to grow, which means you're doing a good job. I heard you're working alone so I hired a friend of a friend to help you out. His name is Stoney, he'll meet you at the Hog Creek Boat Landing tomorrow morning. I think you'll like him." Hiding my apprehension, I thanked him and hung up.

The following morning I met Stoney. He was a sturdy man, medium height, early forties, with a weathered face and a Texas accent. I told him how we had to juggle vehicles, and he was more than willing to help in every way. We tied the boat at the landing and drove separate vehicles to Ennis where we left my truck before returning in his van to the boat landing. I took my place at the oars while Stoney shoved us off. He sprung over the bow with a youthful leap that carried him in what seemed one fluid motion to a sitting position on the bench seat in front of the pump.

We pulled into the eddy at the first film site. Stoney needed no instruction on the pump. He seemed an old hand, knowing more about the operation than I did, and he insisted that I let him handle the watering side of the job while I concentrated on getting us down the river.

"I hate going down this next riffle," I said as we cast off from the second film site.

"Don't do it then!" came his response.

He rolled with the ups and downs, jerks and sways like a bareback horseman enjoying the ride. When the water slowed to a monotonous flow he pulled a coiled 3/8 nylon lasso from his coat, whirled it above his head and tossed the looped end twenty feet in front of the boat. To my surprise a merganser duck bolted in front of the bow with the lasso around its neck.

The merganser carried the rope skyward and flew in a circle like a kite on a string, quacking as it went, until Stoney reeled it in and released it. As the merganser flew away I found myself doubting the reality of what I had just witnessed, but merganser lassoing became a common occurrence and my scale of things that shocked and amazed me diminished by one.

*

As the weeks passed Stoney proved reliable, and the new grass testified that we were a pretty good team. My jitters subsided, and I began to look forward to the rapids. I knew where the rocks were, and instead of concentrating on aiming the bow downstream, I focused on the angle of the stern, backing the boat this way and that to slow it and maneuver around the rocks.

Sam Welch

Each morning before work I stopped and had breakfast at the Applegate Restaurant in Woodville.

The morning cook was lovely, blond and slim, and an excellent cook as well. She brought my breakfast out personally, visiting briefly before returning to the grille. Our conversations seldom slipped beyond, how I liked my eggs, or what I was doing on the river. Her interest flattered me, although I would never have involved myself in anything more than a casual smile and conversation.

Breakfasts lacked flavor on her days off, but I reminded myself that it was about nourishment and completing the job.

One morning Stoney and I were nearing the third film site at Taylor Creek, when I noticed my breakfast cook floating on a nearby rubber raft along with several other people. She rose to her feet smiling and pulled off her sweatshirt revealing her beautiful body clad only in a string bikini. Clasping her hands over her head she dove headlong into the water. When she surfaced I waved and smiled. I would have stopped and talked, but one of the guys in the raft seemed to be glaring at me so I thought better of it.

Stoney turned and cast me an astonished look. "Do you know her?"

"She's my breakfast cook," I replied.

"I'll bet you think she pulled that sweatshirt off just because you were rowing by. Huh?"

"No, the thought never crossed my mind," I lied.

"Uh huh!" He nodded twice and turned back facing downstream as if to suggest that the incident had passed like the flow of the current, but I could almost hear the wheels turning in his mind.

*

One night I received a call from Fred, the Art Director. He had visited the film sites earlier that day.

"You're doing an incredible job Sam but we have a problem, and I was hoping you might be able to help us out with it." "Sure, what is it?" I asked.

"Well, the grass at the Taylor Creek film site has grown too high. The cast and crew will be returning from Montana in three weeks. If we wait till then and mow it the site will look groomed, and we don't want that because it's supposed to be wild and scenic. We need to have someone go in there and cut it now so it will look natural in three weeks. I realize that you don't have time personally but I thought you might know someone who has their own boat and a weed eater to do that for us."

My dive partner, George came to mind. "As a matter of fact I do know someone," I said, "he has an ocean kayak and he could use my weed eater. I'll give him a call. How much does the job pay?"

"Offer him a hundred bucks," Fred replied.

"Okay, I'll give him a call and I'll let you know what he says."

I hung up the phone and dialed George. The phone rang twice and George picked up.

"Hello!"

"Hello George," I replied.

"Hello, hello…"

"Hello George?"

"Hello, hello…"

I realized we had a bad connection. He couldn't hear me. This had happened before, and I assumed the problem was on his end of the line.

"Listen you son of a bitch!" he shouted, "I told you once not to ever prank call me, and if it happens again I'll come right thru this phone line and beat you till you're dead!" A clank and silence followed.

"George, George?" There was no answer so I gave up and redialed.

George picked up and in an angry voice growled, "Hello!"

"Hi George, can you hear me now?"

"Sam!"

"You don't need to kill me George. I won't prank call ya'
again!" We both broke into laughter.

"What's up Sam?"

"How'd you like to make a hundred bucks?" I asked.

"My body's not as beautiful as it used to be!"

"Cutting grass, George! All ya' gotta' do is cut some grass!"

"Darn! I thought you knew some cute chick who was looking for a
guy!
Okay! So where's this grass?"

"Taylor Creek, just below Indian Mary Park. You could take a weed
eater and a can of gas on your kayak and make an easy hundred bucks.
What do ya' say?" "I'm
game," he replied.

"Good. We'll be floating by Indian Mary around 8:30 tomorrow
morning. Meet us at the Indian Mary boat landing and I'll show you where
to go."

The following morning George was ready and waiting. He launched
his kayak and followed us from Indian Mary to Taylor Creek. Stoney and
I watered the site and moved on leaving George behind to cut the grass.
That evening I called George to find out how it went.

"I finished the job, but there's a bee's nest in the ground at the top of
the hill. Yellow Jackets! They stung me sixteen times, chased me right
into the water, waited for me to surface and stung me again! I thought I
was gonna' die!"

"Oh man, I'm sorry George! Hope you're feeling better soon, I'll talk
to the Art Director and get your money, and I'll see what he wants to do
about those bees."

The next morning when we stopped to water the Taylor Creek film
site I found the bee's nest in the ground at the top of the knoll. On my
way home I stopped by Fred's office. I asked his secretary if he was in,
and if I could see him. Fred heard me and came to the outer office. His

smile and greeting was a pleasant contrast to the cold reception his secretary had offered.

"Hi Sam." He shook my hand heartily. "You've probably come to pick up the money for your friend."

"Yes, and there's something else too."

"Come on into the office." He motioned as he rounded the desk. "I'll get your money."

I followed, leaving the door open behind me.

He pulled a grey metal box from his desk drawer, labeled "petty cash," and asked, "and what's the 'something else' you mentioned?"

"Bees! We got bees!"

"Bees?"

"Yes, there's a nest of yellow jackets at Taylor Creek. My friend George got stung sixteen times."

"How do the bees present a problem for us?" he asked.

"Well," I searched my mind for a quick answer. "Suppose Meryl Streep gets stung?"

"Say no more." He raised his right hand to silence me while he counted out a hundred dollars with the other hand. "Do you know someone who could exterminate those bees?"

"Sure, I could take care of it."

He handed me George's money, and clasping his hands in front of him asked, "and how much do you want for that?"

"It ought a' be worth fifty bucks," I replied.

"And how will you do it?"

I leaned forward and whispered with my *if I tell ya' I'll have to kill ya' expression,* "I'll swim in at night with a can of gas, a covert operation you understand, and douse 'em whilst they sleep!"

"That's interesting." He chuckled. "You go ahead and do that, I want to hear all about it, and I hope your friend gets better."

Later that night I drove to the park across from Taylor Creek. I took a dive flashlight and a small can of gasoline and swam across the river.

Sam Welch

When I found the bee's nest I doused it with about two cups of gas and sealed the hole with dirt.

The following day after work I dropped by Fred's office. His secretary met me in the outer office and asked me to wait at her desk. She knocked and entered Fred's office, closing the door behind her.

I could hear her venting to Fred, "We don't even know if there were any bees to begin with. This guy seems like a shyster, and he just made an easy
$50 bucks by inventing a bee's nest!"

The door opened and she came out, releasing an angry sigh. "He'll see you now," she growled.

Fred cast me a suspicious look as I entered. "Did you take care of the bees?" he asked.

"Yep, I did!"

He opened his desk drawer, and after pulling out the petty cash box, began to count out the bills.

I couldn't help the uneasy feeling that came over me. I wanted to convince him of my honesty but that wasn't in the cards, so I decided a little bullshit might smooth things over. "Fred, when I was a kid they offered a bounty on coyotes, but before you could receive that eight dollar bounty you had to bring in a pair of coyote ears. I'd like to prove that I killed those bees, but they have such itty-bitty ears!"

Fred's eyes enlarged, he leaned forward in his chair, seemingly holding his breath until he had handed me the cash, then suddenly he burst out in mixed laughter and coughing.

I thanked him and as I left his office I heard him repeating, "itty bitty ears," over and over followed each time by heavy laughter. I closed the door behind me and realized I was the focus of the secretary's angry glare.

Reaching into my pocket I found several wrapped Hershey's candy. "How 'bout a kiss, baby?" I said as I tossed them on her desk.

As I made my exit her expression never changed, and whether she ate the kisses or discarded them will remain a mystery, but I walked out fifty dollars richer and a million dollars happier.

*

During the final weeks of watering a friend loaned me a boat motor. The motor propelled us rapidly through the long stretches of slow water making our job easier and our work day shorter. We lifted and locked the motor before reaching the riffle where I used the oars to guide us over and around rocks.

Near Ennis Riffle a newlywed couple brought their boat alongside mine. He was an older gentleman, and she an attractive younger woman. Stoney and the old gent shared everything from fishing stories to the weather while the young bride and I sat quietly across from each other in the back of our respective boats. Eventually she struck up a conversation in which she did most of the talking while I listened.

Stopping to chat with the couple became a daily occurrence, and as she grew noticeably more comfortable around me, I became less comfortable around her.

On the final day of their honeymoon, a cold foggy morning, they brought their boat alongside mine for the last time to say their goodbyes. They were going back to California. She wore a frilly orange bikini, and I couldn't help thinking how cold she must have been.

While the old man and Stoney caught up on jokes and weather she told me how happy she was to have met me. I exchanged a couple of "you toos," and a "goodbye" before shoving off feeling it was none too soon.

Moments later Stoney broke the silence, "I'll bet you think she wore that skimpy little bikini just for you!"

"I never gave it a thought!" I blurted so quick on the heels of his comment that he must have realized that I knew what he was going to say.

"Yeah, you did. You thought she wore that just for you!"

"It is a little cold for a bikini," I reasoned, hoping he'd leave it at that.

"Wearing a bikini on a morning like this is dumber than a box of rocks," he agreed, adding, "but the point is you think that every girl wants you. Admit it, you do!"

"I confess, every girl wants me. But can you blame them?" I chuckled knowing my admission would end the argument and bring final closure to Stoney's assumption.

*

Shellie shook her head and gave me that half-smile reserved for hopeless cases like me, and after a sigh she said, "I still want to hear about Meryl Streep. She's my favorite actress! I've watched her on talk shows and I just love her. Did you meet her? What's she like?"

"Well, she's a little different in person…"

Chapter Twenty

After the cast and crew returned to the area Josh asked Stoney and I to stay on as laborers. He said there were things that aren't included in the union grip's job description like setting up tents, loading and unloading boats, and moving portable outhouses, or 'blue rooms,' and a myriad of other tasks that needed done.

The cast and crew set up for shooting on the sandbar below Hellgate where Hog Creek meets the Rogue.

I was given a rake to smooth the footprints out of the sand after every take. The idea was to make the sand look as though it had not been walked on. Occasionally we moved a log or a tent to suit the directors. Measurements and pictures were taken after every change so that the scene could be duplicated inside a large building that had been selected as a studio.

Meryl was not as tall nor as attractive as she seemed in the movies although I thought she had nice legs.

I avoided looking at her. I didn't want her to think I was star-stricken, but I couldn't escape her unmistakable angry glare, and I thought perhaps she had me confused with someone else, someone she didn't like.

Later that afternoon Stoney and I were setting up the large cafeteria tent in the parking lot above Hog Creek boat landing when we noticed we had company.

Meryl was watching us. She was crouched in a squatting position smoking a cigarette merely thirty feet away. I wondered how she could be entertained watching two men in an empty parking lot setting up a tent.

I couldn't help feeling uneasy, partly because of her gaze, and partly because I could hear the wheels turning in Stoney's mind.

"She want's you dude!"

"Quiet she can hear you!" I forced through clenched teeth.

"She really wants you!" He chuckled.

"Your kidding is not funny right now!" I snapped.

"I'm not kidding. Look at that expression, she wants you!"

"I'm not gonna' look. Tell me when she's gone."

Stoney had no problem positioning every rope and strut, releasing an annoying chuckle every few seconds, while I struggled to keep my mind on the job, stumbling over my own nerves.

Meryl remained our audience through, what must have taken several cigarettes. She left as we were putting the finishing touches on the tent, and only then was I able to breathe freely.

The following morning Josh had me loading and unloading boats on a new dock that the Jet Boat Company had installed at the Hog Creek Boat Landing. The dock was a large floating platform secured by cables that were anchored in the hillside above.

Stoney was working elsewhere, which afforded me a break from his kidding. My work was laidback except for heavy lifting to which I was accustomed, and I felt somewhat relaxed.

Bacon strode onto the dock where he greeted us. He abruptly dropped to the deck and hammered out thirty quick pushups before jumping sprightly onto the cast boat.

John C. Reilley followed. He seemed personable and polite, and I was later to learn that he was enamored with rockets. In his free time he loved to launch bottle rockets and the like.

David Strathairn was next. Among the actors, I admired him the most. He was intelligent, witty, polite and humble. I had seen him in films in supporting rolls, and I felt ashamed and disadvantaged when he addressed me as "Sam", and I didn't know his name. He was never too good to join with laborers and crew over a card game or lunch, and I couldn't help thinking that the film industry would have been perfect if all the actors were like him.

I was standing by the side of the cast boat when Meryl showed up. My first instinct was to run and hide, but I stood my ground, avoiding eye contact. She leaned against me and rested her head on my shoulder. I was more than mildly unnerved, and in desperation I searched my mind for the proper response.

"Do you need a hand getting on the boat?" I extended my arm, and blurted, in a voice that sounded froggy when I played it back in my mind.

She stepped back looking me up and down as if to size me up, and then she jumped onto the boat with a single athletic stride.

As the boat pulled away one of the boat drivers who was standing on the dock came over. "That rotten bitch did the same thing to me yesterday!" he said.

"Really! Why that two-timing hussy! And I thought I was the only one!" I sighed, feigning disappointment in order to make light of the situation. The truth is I was still a bit shaken. "Nope, join the crowd." He chuckled. "I'll never offer her my hand again!" "Neither will I," he said.

*

The next day around lunch time I was working on the same dock when the cast boat returned from the film site.

Bacon was seated cross legged on the bow and Meryl was leaning against the stern.

Bacon stood and tossed me the bow rope. I pulled the boat to the dock but as I bent over to tie it to the cleat Bacon jumped over my head. The thrust from his jump coupled with the fast movement of the river forced the boat away from the dock. I stood up to pull the boat back in and noticed Meryl looking at me as she came up through the canvas cabin, a smirk on her face. I realized she intended to jump over my head as well.

I pulled the boat in with all my strength and bent to tie it to the cleat. After three quick half hitches and a rushed granny I stood to my feet hoping to get out of her way. I was too late. She was already in mid stride, and I stood up right between her legs.

She balanced for a moment on my shoulder like a gymnast on a pommel horse, her butt against my cheek. I felt her start to slip and I

163

threw my arm up to keep her from falling but she flung her leg over my arm and slid down my back. My arm lodged, shoulder deep in a slit in the back of her jacket which twisted tight around my armpit.

She landed at a brisk walk, and I, unable to free myself from her jacket was jerked off balance. I found myself running backwards, head to head with her to keep from falling over.

"Wait, wait! Let me get my arm out," I begged, but she refused to stop.

After regaining my footing, a grunting groaning tug-of-war ensued and I was able finally to slide her jacket from my arm and free myself.

I didn't turn around, I didn't want to see her I just faced the water. I felt humiliated and out-gunned. I didn't know what she was thinking, and I didn't care.

*

"What! Are you kidding me?" Shellie blurted.

"You probably think I'm making this up as I go, right?" I didn't care if she believed me, I was ready to surrender and end the story anyway.

She motioned with her hands frantically palms out as if to say she didn't want me to think like that. "No, no, this is far too crazy for anyone to make up. Not even you could make this up. This has to be true!"

I was reeling from the "Not even you…" when she reached out and grabbed my hands, begging, "Go on, please go on, I've got to hear this!"

"Awright," I conceded. I cleared my throat and continued.

*

Josh asked my advice. He wanted to invent a harness for carrying blue rooms (portable outhouses) to and from the isolated film sites via helicopter. He had a system of cables that extended from the base of each blue room with four lines that connected to a single ring on top. When they tested it the blue rooms swayed and tipped. He also needed a safe means of connecting and disconnecting from the helicopter cable.

I suggested adding an additional harness around the top of each unit, and an overhead rack to prevent sway.

164

For connecting and disconnecting I recommended carabiner hooks which I had learned to use during repelling exercises in Navy Seal Training. Josh took my advice and the new system worked well.

The Ennis Riffle film site was deemed inadequate and a new site had to be selected.

A third location manager was brought in from the Jurassic Park movie. He took over most of Josh's duties, and became my new boss. I often accompanied him scouting for film locations. He relied heavily on my advice, and I found him likeable.

We moved camp from Hog Creek Boat Landing to Almeda Park which meant a lot of extra hours for Stoney and I, moving and setting up tents and blue rooms.

A new makeup girl joined the crew. She was beautiful and friendly. Meryl gave me an angry glare when she saw us talking. I couldn't be certain that it was any different from Meryl's normal angry glare, and connecting the dots was impossible, but the following day I learned that my newfound-friend had been transferred to second unit.

Lunch time usually found me at the same table with the same group of people. Bacon often sat across from me. He was an interesting conversationalist with prolific, even creative usage of words that some would call profanity. He was from Connecticut and entertained a future in politics. He and his wife, who was also an actor, and present during the filming, had considered buying a house in Southern Oregon, but the local press wouldn't leave them alone which made him think better of it.

There were two ladies who worked as flaggers directing traffic during filming. They often joined me for lunch and since they were local fish like myself in a sea of outsiders, they seemed to add an air of home cooking to the conversation. One of the women had a son who went to school with my daughter, and I felt at home around them.

The flaggers told me that Meryl had tried to have them transferred to second unit, but since they worked for the road department her demands were denied.

165

Sam Welch

Meryl often snuck up behind me and bumped me in the back with her lunch tray. There was always a producer or director standing nearby to shout, "What's wrong with you, idiot, get out of her way!"

I learned quickly to avoid pathways and walkways when she was around, which enabled me to point to the walkway and defend myself with, "I'm not in her way! The walkway is there!"

One day she was running a foot race against the child actor who played her son on the set.

An audience of perhaps a hundred cast and crew cheered them on. I was amazed at how quick and agile she was until she abandoned the race, veering from the beaten path in my direction. She stopped abruptly chest to chest with me and even though she bumped me only mildly she caused me to spill a hot cup of noodles onto my forearm. I'm not sure which burned more, the noodles or her gaze as she stood for a moment glaring up into my face while the crowd shouted at me, "get out of her way!"

A hush fell over cast and crew each time she spoke, a sudden and uncanny silence replacing the clamor as if life's existence hinged on her every word. Sometimes she sang, always an Abba song, always with perfect rhythm. Her voice was beautiful making me wonder why she chose acting over singing.

Deputies from the local sheriff's department and the Sheriff himself served as security on the set during their off hours, and I became well acquainted with most of them.

One of the makeup men, Jay always greeted me with a smile. He was about six foot five, and more than mildly effeminate, but I, being a beggar and not a chooser when it comes to friendship have always liked those who like me, and I had no reason not to like Jay, until I felt his interest in me might be going beyond casual friendship.

Jay was a black belt in karate, and an accomplished actor as well. He always had a positive attitude, and he told interesting stories about behindthe-scenes movie making.

The deputies that I hung out with excused themselves with, "Oh hell, here comes that faggot!" when Jay approached.

I saw their actions as rude, and on one occasion I caught John, one of the deputies by the arm and kept him from leaving. "John, have you met Jay?" I asked, as I gesticulated, adding, "Jay—John, John—Jay!"

Jay was summoned on the set, and after offering John a washrag handshake, and a girlish, "pleased to meet you, John," he hurried away.

John turned to me, wiping his hand on his pants almost obsessively and growled, "How could you? How could you do that to me?"

I could only laugh, but I knew I'd better not let John catch me speeding on a county road after that.

*

On a warm night in late August we moved back to Hog Creek to redo a birthday scene. The move was sudden and rushed. Stoney and I worked through the night moving tents, tables and blue rooms. The hectic scheduling seemed to take a toll on Meryl as well and by the next evening her voice had become raspy and hoarse as she performed take after take singing "happy birthday."

There was a sandy knoll fifty yards from the set surrounded by a forest of willows, the perfect place for a nap.

I told Stoney where I'd be, and asked him to wake me when they wrapped.

The knoll was far enough from the noise of the set and the glare of the huge spotlights on the cliffs above to give me the peace and quiet I needed to fall asleep.

"It's 2:20 A.M!" Stoney shook my shoulder.

I sat upright and yawned. Several hours had slipped by in the wink of an eye.

"It's a wrap! You'd better catch a boat out now, unless you want to stay here and swim out in the morning." Stoney chuckled as he turned and walked away.

I sat there for a moment yawning, seriously considering staying and swimming out. A rustle in the willows caught my attention. A moment later Meryl stood over me, her hands on her hips, her expression, angry. "Do you have any Idea what time it is?" she demanded.

In a groggy stupor I glanced at my wrist. "No, I don't have my watch," I replied.

Her expression changed from anger to pity. She sighed, shook her head and turned to leave.

"No wait, someone just told me it's 2:20 A.M." I blurted.

She turned back and gave me an open mouth you-must-be-crazy, I'll-burn-a-hole-in-you glare before turning again to walk away.

I sat for a moment recalling my words, wondering what I had said that seemed so stupid.

"Someone just told me it's 2:20 A.M.," Oh shit! She thinks I hear voices!

I knew from that moment sleep would be impossible so I got up and caught a boat out.

*

"How do you think she found you?" Shellie asked.

"I didn't think about it at the time, but I realized later that she followed Stoney." I replied.

"Unbelievable!" Shellie said. She shook her head and reached out to touch my hand, "I don't mean I don't believe you. I do believe you. I just mean it's unbelievable. Well, you know what I mean."

"Yeah!" I shook my head, and then nodded and shook my head again to poke fun at her statement.

She laughed. "Please tell me more."

*

Dr. Jones made a house call to the set carrying a black leather medical bag. Accompanying him, one on either side, were two nurses wearing traditional white nurse uniforms and hats. One of the grips cracked a joke about making a porn movie, but it turned out that Meryl's soar throat had worsened and Jones was there to check it out.

I knew Dr. Jones outside the office—we worked out at the same fitness club where we shared bullshit and exchanged an occasional joke, but his house call on the set forever changed the image that pops into my mind when I think of him.

Jones made only one visit to the set, but Meryl's voice was back in no time and the movie—back on track. I could only assume that whatever he had in his bag worked.

*

We moved the camp to Indian Mary Park and began filming at Taylor Creek. The jet boats ferried us back and forth at meal times and after each wrap.

The scenery was nicer—Indian Mary with its manicured lawns and tall trees and Taylor Creek with its grassy knoll overlooking the film site contributed to a more laid back atmosphere.

The grips installed a fake creek and waterfall at Taylor Creek. The water for the fake creek was pumped from the river onto the hillside and channeled over a large rock. I thought it lacked realism, but the cast and crew liked it.

Jay was becoming manipulative, controlling and possessive. I wanted to find a way to avoid him without becoming his enemy. I found myself hoping that someone else would catch his fancy and that he would leave me alone, but extinguishing his man crush and going back to casual friends was not a smooth transition.

"Where's a good breakfast restaurant?" he asked.

"I like the Applegate in Woodville," I told him.

"Good! Meet me there at six A. M. tomorrow morning."

"I won't be there, Jay!" I said, wondering how the taste of raw foot had so effortlessly made its way to my palate.

"You'd better be there!" He looked and sounded offended.

"I won't be there Jay!"

"Why won't you be there?"

"Because it sounds like a date and I don't want to go on a date with you!"

"Be there, or you'll be sorry!" He warned.

"Why, what are you going to do if I don't show up?"

"You'll see," he nodded with a pseudo smile and anger in his eyes, adding, "and you'll be sorry!"

I felt mixed relief and uneasiness as he stomped away, and I tried to dismiss the incident from my mind by watching the repeated takes of the fight scene between Bacon and Strathairn.

Between the takes Fred arrived on the set. When he wasn't busy I caught his attention. "If you have a minute I'd like to show you something."

"Sure Sam."

I led him onto the knoll where I kicked at the ground exposing the hive of dead yellow jackets.

"Sam, you didn't have to show me this. I never doubted you for a minute."

"I felt like I needed to prove that I'm not a shyster," I said.

"Not to me you don't!" He bent down and carefully took one of the dead bees by the wing. Straightening, he held it up in the sunlight and examined it. "I see no ears!" he said.

"Oh they have 'em, they're just itty-bitty!" I nodded in the most affirming manner I could muster.

"Well then I'll have to take your word for it." He flicked the bee from his fingers adding, "I've got to get back to the office. Have a good day Sam."

*

I was on the set at Taylor Creek early the following morning.

After a few tasks I went atop the knoll to escape the bustle of cast and crew as they set up their equipment.

Around seven A.M. Jay arrived. As soon as he stepped ashore he scoured the area visually. When he spotted me, he began waving both arms, jumping up and down while shouting at the top of his lungs, "Sam, oh

Sam!"

A hush fell over the crowd as he continued with, "I'm so sorry, I forgot all about our date!"

Every eye turned and focused on me. The silence morphed into mild chatter followed by scattered laughter that ever-too-slowly slipped back to the normal sound of the work day grind.

In the days and weeks that followed I found myself turning down one male pass after another, telling them "I'm not gay!"

*

Shellie burst into childish laughter, covering her mouth with her hand.

"Stop it! Stop it!" I motioned sheepishly in a soft high voice with a mild lisp.

When she caught her breath she said, "It sounds like you finally got in touch with your feminine side."

"Yeth I dit, but my masculine appeal hath never wavered!"

She chuckled again and asked, "Did they ever put you in the movie?"

I returned to my normal voice, "As a matter of fact they put me in three times but edited me out twice. I'm still in one spot but if you blink you'll miss it. Meryl and Dave are rowing down river plotting how they're going to get their son back when I walk down the river bank in the background." "That sounds simple," she said.

"It wasn't that simple—they did five takes!"

*

The grips had built a campfire high on the riverbank using a propane torch to burn waterlogged driftwood which burned poorly creating billows of smoke. I was instructed to stand facing the fire until I was given the cue to walk down to the river's edge.

The smoke from the fire oozed into my face choking me and burning my eyes. When my cue came I started down the river bank. Meryl and Dave were rowing past, their lines were perfect.

Suddenly I heard the director shouting from across the river, "Cut, cut! I can see tears in that fisherman's eyes from here, and if I can see it through the camera the viewers will see it on film. Now take him back up there and let's roll again."

While a jet boat towed the raft back up river, I took my place by the fire.

A second and third take brought the same outcome, with the director growing more impatient each time.

The fourth take found me praying the wind would change, but when it didn't I took my cue and started down the bank.

"Cut, cut!" the director exploded, "All I want is for that fisherman to walk down the bank without crying! What's so hard about that?"

Pointing to the campfire, I shouted back with almost as much venom, "You've got me standing in the smoke, and you expect me not to cry?"

"Okay, okay," he shouted, "Grips do something about that smoke! I don't care if you have to put a fan on it, but get it out of his face!"

The fifth and final take was a keeper, and I was happy to see my brief film debut end.

*

We moved the camp again to Almeda, and continued filming just below Argo Riffle.

I was working on the Almeda set when Meryl's husband came looking for her.

"Hide me, I don't want to see him," I heard her say as she stepped behind me, pressing her body close against my back, while clenching my sweatshirt tightly in her fists. The cast and crew grew silent as he wondered about.

He was a pleasant looking man, average height and build with a touch of grey on the sides of his otherwise brown hair, and I could hear my heart beating through my chest as he neared and asked if anyone had seen her.

I thought about what I should say if he discovered Meryl hiding behind me and confronted me. *Were there words for this sort of thing?* If so it would be better un-rehearsed.

Some of the wardrobe people crowded in to help conceal her. One of the women struck up a conversation with me, "I thought I heard her say she forgot something back at camp!" A ruse, no doubt to avert suspicion and tame what must have been my "Barney Fife" in-the-headlights expression. Her words came across as strange and meaningless to me and I could only shrug my shoulders and nod. Acting was never my forte.

One of the producers offered, "I don't know! She was here earlier! Maybe she's in one of the blue rooms!"

Meryl's husband wandered about for several more agonizing minutes before getting back on the cast boat and leaving.

Within moments everything was back to normal on the set, but it took more than an hour to calm my restless nerves.

*

"Are you kidding me?" Shellie's question was almost a statement.

"No!" I nodded trying to appear as serious as possible.

The waitress was back, holding two menus against her apron. "Would you like to see our lunch menu?" she asked politely.

"I'm still not hungry, thankyou, although I'll take a refill on my Coke," I told her.

"How about you, ma'am?"

Shellie glanced at her glass and swirled the small amount of Coke in the bottom. "I'll just have a refill on the Coke too, please," she said.

"Okay then, I'll be right back with two more Cokes." The waitress nodded and smiled as she turned to walk away.

Shellie leaned forward, a serious expression on her face. "Where were we? Go on with your story."

*

The make was GM, a 1977 three quarter ton long bed pickup. I can't tell you the color, I'm terrible that way, although I think it was tan.

I noticed it darting in and out of traffic in my rear view mirror on the north-bound lane of I-5 just North of Grants Pass.

My first thought was that someone crazy was driving.

I was doing around eighty in my Ford Bronco II when she passed me on the right.

Meryl was driving, and the woman who served as nanny for her youngest child was riding shotgun. I found myself taken aback for a moment, since an old pickup was the last thing I expected to see her in.

She had barely cleared my front bumper when she whipped in front of me and slammed on the brakes.

I hit my brakes and skidded to keep from rear ending her. She sped up, leaving me behind, although she eventually pulled into the right lane and slowed.

I merged into the right lane several vehicles behind her and maintained the same speed as the cars around me, intending to keep a buffer and a safe distance between our two vehicles.

She slowed again to around forty miles per hour and I joined the line of cars that went around her while cautiously watching her in my rear view mirror.

After passing a few more cars and realizing that the road lay open ahead of me, I floored the pedal and widened the distance between us. I was all but certain she could never catch up when I noticed her gaining on me rapidly, and I couldn't help but wonder what she had under the hood of that truck.

She passed me as though I were standing still and once again whipped in front of me and slammed on the brakes. I braked and swerved narrowly missing her back bumper.

That was enough for me, I pulled over to the side of the freeway and stopped, thinking that if I couldn't outrun her I could out-wait her.

She stopped on the shoulder ahead of me and waited. It seemed like a long wait, several minutes I suppose, but finally she drove away.

I found her waiting for me again near the Merlin off-ramp, and I stayed behind her until she rolled up to the stop sign. She lingered there until angry motorists who were backed up on the freeway began to honk. When she pulled out again I remained behind her, keeping my distance until I reached the camp.

*

Shellie shook her head and sighed. "I would have given her a piece of my mind, but I don't suppose you ever did."

I shook my head, realizing my lack of testicular fortitude had been exposed, "no, I never did, although I thought I might write about it someday, but there's a fat chance of that. I haven't seriously written anything in…well, in more than nineteen years."

"That's right, I had forgotten, you were going to be a writer." A sad smile formed on her face and she nodded slowly as if sifting through gloomy memories. "I can't understand why you never pursued it."

I shrugged and tried to smile, not wanting to let on that she might have had anything to do with it, although I couldn't help but ponder how fragile the human mind is, or how it can be so easily destroyed by failed love.

I raised my Coke and broke the moment's silence with, "my life sounds like an old Harry Chapin song!" I released a sad chuckle and continued, "It's nice to have youthful dreams, and even better if you can pursue them, but if they don't pan out its good if you can shrug and say, 'I guess it wasn't in the cards,' and move on."

She raised her glass and touched it to mine, and smiling said, "here's to youthful dreams. As life moves on may they always pan out!" After a sip she set her glass down and continued, "So you never gave her a piece of your mind!"

"I knew you wouldn't let that go!" I took a drink and swallowed. "Meryl and I never spoke after that. Sometimes she cast me a casual smile or a stern defiant expression when we passed. I didn't try to read her, she is too good of an actress. I still don't know what her motives were in harassing me, I suppose she simply enjoyed making me stutter, and I'm sure there's at least one like me on the set of every movie she's ever made. If I had to describe her in one word I would say mischievous!" I took another sip and continued, "Earlier this week when we finally rapped after the last shoot on the river Meryl boarded the cast boat and called out to the rest of us on shore, 'I'm glad it's over, I can't wait to get out of this hellhole and back to civilization!' I couldn't help feeling insulted, this 'hellhole' being my home." "Well yeah!" Shellie protested.

I straightened in my chair and breathed a sigh, "Okay, I've shared my life's story, but you haven't told me anything about yourself." I pointed my index finger at her. "It's your turn! Tell me about you."

A sadness fell over Shellie's face. She blinked several times, shook her head and shrugged. "There's not really much to tell. I think you met Steve." "Yes I think I did." I nodded.

"Steve and I married." She reached up and wiped a tear from under her eye, and continued, "We were married fifteen years and had two daughters." Her speech seemed to slow as she struggled for words between breaths and sobs. "One day Steve said he didn't want to be married anymore. He moved out and moved in with the woman next door! Every morning when I'm doing dishes I watch him through the window as he carries his lunch pail onto the front porch. She follows him there, and they kiss. It rips my heart out!" She covered her face with her hands and began to cry uncontrollably.

A lump formed in my throat, it hurt to see her cry, this long lost friend, the woman I would have married.

She pulled her hands from her face and angrily blurted, "She's thirty eight years old, and she's fat and ugly!"

The awkwardness of her outburst took me by surprise, and I didn't know how to respond. It wasn't funny, but I clenched my tongue in my teeth to ensure I wouldn't laugh. She too was thirty eight and youth and beauty had escaped her.

I handed her some napkins and continued to pat her arm feeling as though the moment begged for a response. "I wish I could say 'I know how you feel,' but nothing like that has ever happened to me… except when you…" I paused, wishing I had kept my mouth shut.

She removed her hands from her tear-strewn reddened face. Slobber formed a string between her lips as she spoke, "I always felt like I made a horrible mistake!"

The lump moved higher in my throat. I too choked back tears. "It's all just water under the bridge now, and we'll both be okay." I said.

I patted her elbow and handed her more napkins. Her tears seemed to be subsiding when she asked, "What really prompted you to call after all these years?"

I cleared and began, "I was sitting in church. The guest speaker was a missionary from Africa. I'd never seen him before, and he knew nothing about me, so when he stopped in mid-sermon to tell me that I needed to forgive the girl who dumped me nineteen years ago, I took it as a mandate from God, and here I am."

"It was probably good for both of us." She smiled.

"I think so, I think this is the moment I've unwittingly waited nineteen years for, and it came and went so quickly, it's as if I just sat down, and now it's almost over. Promise me we'll do it again nineteen years from now."

"It's a date!" She smiled again as she daubed her eyes with a napkin. "It's been wonderful to see you. Are you still going to dive?" "I'll make an afternoon dive," I told her.

"I hope your dive partner isn't too put out at you for missing the morning dive, and I hope you get some fish." She added.

"George? Nah! If he is he'll get over it." The mention of diving had aroused a longing in me that could only be quenched by weightlessly gliding through forests of kelp, a hunter in a strange world. I could almost hear the "thunk" of my spear-pole striking the bony plate above the gills of a large lingcod. I could feel the ensuing struggle. My hands were quivering.

The scent of salt air stirred anew in my nostrils, and I had to go.

I rose to my feet. "It's been wonderful," I said.

We exchanged hugs and goodbyes. I paid the tab, and tipped the waitress.

Driving away I felt free from a bond that had held me for nineteen years, a bond that I didn't know I carried.

Later that week I started my first novel, "What's Your Problem, Cowboy?" A satirical spoof possibly inspired by Wilbur and his buddies.

Shortly thereafter I ran into Dr. Jones at the fitness center.

As he mounted the Stairmaster machine beside me I struck up a conversation. "I saw you on the movie set with your medical bag and two nurses."

"Ah yes, how is Mz Streep?" He asked, as he programed the machine and began climbing on the pedals.

"The last time I saw her she was back to her altered state of normal," I joked.

He muttered something that over the loud noise of the Stairmaster sounded like, "the lab never returned the results on the stool sample, so who would know?"

My "excuse me?" received no response, and in my mildly warped imagination I pictured a molding cluster of dung encased and framed on a lab wall while busy technicians walk to and fro seldom giving it a second thought!

The End